Spreading the Feast, b〉 .... ιent
of the sacrament of th ....)ro-
vide an accurate theoloɡɪᴄᴀɪ aɪɪᴅ ᴅɪᴅɪɪᴄᴀɪ foundation for understanding the sacrament, he also balances it with godly pastoral sensitivity. All church leaders and laity will benefit from this book. I now wait eagerly for Dr. Griffith's reflections on baptism.

—PETER LEE, Associate Professor of Old Testament,
Reformed Theological Seminary, Washington, DC

Dr. Howard Griffith writes both as a warm-hearted pastor and as a clear-headed professor. As someone trying to straddle these worlds, I found that *Spreading the Feast* was just what I needed. A dip into these pages immediately offered new and helpful thoughts about the Lord's Supper; a dive into the book has already changed the way in which I celebrate this sacrament with God's people. If you love the written Word and visible Words of God, this book will be a treat!

—CHAD VAN DIXHOORN, Chancellor's Professor of
Historical Theology, Reformed Theological Seminary,
Washington, DC

As a pastor, I've longed to lead our people more deeply into fellowship with Christ at his Table, but have felt limited. Using the entire Scripture to set the Table, and then practical meditations for preparing the meal, Howard Griffith has provided ministers every resource for rightly serving up the rich fare of God's grace.

—GLENN HOBURG, Grace Downtown church,
Washington, DC

This book is for the minister of Word and sacrament. Griffith draws from years of pastoral ministry and biblical study to build this treatment of the Lord's Supper that is eminently usable, deeply redemptive-historical, and beautifully rendered. The young pastor will benefit from early exposure to Griffith's meditations on the table, and the experienced pastor will find refreshment from the expert voice of a peer.

—Scott Redd, President, Associate Professor of
Old Testament, Reformed Theological Seminary,
Washington, DC

Are you a Christian who wonders what you should be thinking about at the Lord's Supper? Or perhaps a pastor at a loss to know how to help your people taste the riches of Christ at Communion? Then *Spreading the Feast* is the book for you. Professor Howard Griffith puts us all in his debt by his clear and rich exposition of the meaning of the Supper. But he does much more than that. Reclaiming the older tradition of "table sermons," he simultaneously provides both a model for pastors and soul-nourishing teaching to help us all to discover the joy of union and communion with Christ. So "taste and see that the Lord is good"!

—Sinclair B. Ferguson, Professor of Systematic Theology,
Redeemer Seminary, Dallas

When my local church asked me to preside at the Lord's Supper once a month, I worried that in time I would run out of ideas. But, as it turned out, the meaning of the Lord's Supper and its applications to the Christian's life and thought are inexhaustible. Every time I prepare an introduction to the communion service I learn something new. I have also learned much from books by other writers about the Lord's Supper. Most recently I have profited greatly from *Spreading the Feast* by my colleague Howard Griffith. Howard begins with a concise Reformed theology of the sacrament, then presents a number of his own table addresses from his long pastoral experience. His treatment is biblically sound, and he opens up rich themes, of which some pastors may be unaware. The book will be very useful for pastors and students of theology. I recommend it highly.

—JOHN M. FRAME, J. D. Trimble Professor of Systematic Theology and Philosophy, Reformed Theological Seminary, Orlando

It's a privilege to commend this able and edifying treatment of the Lord's Supper. Its consideration of the Table's significance, followed by a number of brief meditations stemming from Griffith's own ministering there over the years, is biblically and theologically sound and insightful throughout. Here indeed is a feast for all who value their participation in the sacrament, but especially for pastors, whether beginning or experienced, looking for help in making their own ministering at the Table more meaningful and honoring to the Lord.

—RICHARD B. GAFFIN JR., Professor of Biblical and Systematic Theology, Emeritus, Westminster Theological Seminary, Philadelphia

SPREADING
the FEAST

Dear Virginia,

Thanks very much for your
support of our work at RTS'
Washington. We are deeply
grateful to share this ministry
with you.

Howard Griffith

April 2016

Spreading *the* Feast

Instruction & Meditations
for MINISTRY *at the* LORD'S TABLE

HOWARD GRIFFITH

P&R PUBLISHING

P.O. BOX 817 • PHILLIPSBURG • NEW JERSEY 08865-0817

ISBN: 978-1-62995-176-8 (pbk)

ISBN: 978-1-62995-177-5 (ePub)

ISBN: 978-1-62995-178-2 (Mobi)

All Reformed confessions cited in the book are taken from the text of Mid-America Reformed Seminary, *Ecumenical and Reformed Creeds and Confessions* (Orange City, IA: Mid-America Reformed Seminary, 1991).

Quotes from Calvin's *Institutes* in the book are taken from John Calvin, *Institutes of the Christian Religion*, ed. John T. McNeill, trans. Ford Lewis Battles, 2 vols., Library of Christian Classics 20–21 (Philadelphia: Westminster, 1960). They are cited in the notes in the following format: *Inst.*, vol.:page (book/chapter.section).

Printed in the United States of America

Library of Congress Cataloging-in-Publication Data

Griffith, Howard, 1954-
  Spreading the feast : instruction and meditations for ministry at the Lord's table / Howard Griffith.
    pages cm
  ISBN 978-1-62995-176-8 (pbk.) — ISBN 978-1-62995-177-5 (epub) — ISBN 978-1-62995-178-2 (mobi)
  1. Lord's Supper. I. Title.
  BV825.3.G75 2015
  234'.163—dc23
              2015033765

To Jackie,
my love, "heirs together of the grace of life."

Contents

List of Meditations

The Riches of Union with Christ

Introduction

The Lord's Supper has a central place in the life of every believer. God has placed it there, along with the ministry of the Word and baptism. Our Savior, Jesus Christ, promises to meet us and share fellowship with us at his Table. Yet too often, because of a lack of attention, the Supper does not have the richness and beauty due to it as the sign and seal of our union with the resurrected Christ. I hope to help the church to refocus its attention on our communion with Christ at the Supper by answering this question: how *should* we minister at the Lord's Table? As a pastor or leader, whether your church has a set liturgy for the Supper or not, you will need to guide God's people to look to him in faith and love as they commune with Christ at the Table. I provide here biblical Invitations and Meditations that will help you to build up the body of Christ to receive him at his covenant meal. God has "spread the feast" for his people, but it is your task also to do this. As you minister these "visible words" in faith, the body of Christ will be built up.

From its first worship service in June 1984, our newly planted church in Richmond, Virginia, observed the Lord's Supper. Gathered first and foremost to hear Christ's written Word, we also understood the Supper as a part of the ministry of the Word and believed that we should receive it as often as possible. The New Testament does not require the church to observe the Lord's Supper every week. But there is significant precedent for it in the Reformed tradition, and the leadership of our young church wanted to try it.[1] There was no

---

1 Hughes Oliphant Old details the history of the Reformed churches' practice of the Supper in his massive study, *Holy Communion in the Piety of the Reformed Church*, ed. Jon D. Payne (Powder Springs, GA: Tolle Lege Press, 2013).

looking back! We ate and drank every week for the twenty-three years of my ministry there and were never sorry. God met us and nourished our faith.

Most of my efforts as a pastor have been given to preaching, the exposition and application of Holy Scripture. I believe in the power of the Holy Spirit working by and with the Word in the hearts of his people.[2] I believe that the sacraments were given, not as a substitute for the Word, but to enhance and seal the Word to our faith.[3] Christ gave us the Supper, wrote John Calvin, "to awaken, arouse, stimulate, and exercise the feeling of faith and love, and indeed, to correct the defect of both."[4]

At the same time, once we had decided to observe the Supper every week, to be honest, I feared that the congregation might become bored. Gordon-Conwell Theological Seminary was a place of outstanding instruction in Holy Scripture and Reformed theology. I grew in knowledge of the Christ of Scripture there. But I received very little instruction in the theology of the sacraments and almost no practice in conducting worship.[5] At All Saints Reformed Presbyterian Church, I feared that the Lord's Table could become a rote, empty observance, something less than a means of God's grace. My experience since then has reinforced that concern. In many churches the Lord's Table is, in a way, silent. God always speaks through his Word, including this Word, but in too many places the Supper is a brief "add-on." Sometimes the liturgy is unexamined, or the words of institution are even omitted altogether. This tends to silence a rich means of God's comfort, assurance, and challenge to the church.

---

2 See Westminster Confession of Faith, 1.5.

3 The word "sacrament" is used throughout to refer to baptism and the Lord's Supper, the two rites instituted by Jesus for use in his church until he returns. If anyone prefers the term "ordinance," that would make no theological difference in the presentation of this book.

4 *Inst.*, 2:1420 (4/17.42).

5 For the most part, this was due to my poor "theological eyesight." I had been nurtured in the Christian life by outstanding mentors, but largely outside the life of the church.

In seminary I read the "Table Addresses" of Professor John Murray, delivered in his pastoral ministry in the Scottish Highlands.[6] John Murray's ministry was, to me, the embodiment of Christ-exalting and biblical spirituality, based on his penetrating biblical theology. Murray's exposition of Scripture was both exegetically profound and deeply edifying. In his situation, the ministry of the Lord's Table was quite different than it would be in mine. There were "Communion seasons," lengthy services, administered periodically. By contrast, our church planned to observe Communion each week. I needed to modify what Murray had done, but the principle of giving a specific Meditation seemed sound. As a minister of the Word, I had a responsibility to explain the Lord's meaning in the Supper and to exhort the church to receive the riches of Christ. Christ is the food and drink of his people. He is our life. His Table is a feast. The task of "spreading the feast" for God's people was before me. So, armed with Murray's five "Table Addresses," I set out to minister at the Lord's Table for a lifetime.

We never regretted the decision to observe the Supper weekly. Our God never left us, week by week, without the blessing of communion with Jesus Christ. And, despite very imperfect presentations, there was always (to my amazement!) something important to say in introducing the Lord's Supper.

From that experience, as I continued to study theology, I learned something vital, something I was unaware of as a young minister. The sacraments are as rich in blessings as is the Lord Jesus, whose covenant they seal. Like the New Testament itself, they preach the unsearchable riches of Christ. A growing grasp of the doctrine of union with Christ and of the covenant character of the Bible has caused my understanding of the value of the sacraments to grow dramatically. This is the trajectory of what I learned: Scripture itself is the book by which God

---

6 These marvelous addresses are found in John Murray, *Collected Writings of John Murray*, vol. 3, *The Life of John Murray: Sermons and Reviews*, ed. Iain H. Murray (Edinburgh: Banner of Truth, 1982), 275–88.

administers his covenant. The message of all Scripture is Jesus Christ in his death and resurrection. He is the content and the Mediator of the covenant. Sacraments, in the hand of the Holy Spirit, seal Christ and his grace to believers. By them we grow in faith, hope, and love.

It seemed a good thing to try to write down a number of the "Meditations" that I gave over the years. That project has grown into this book. I offer them with the hope that they may help other ministers (especially young ones) to present the riches of God's grace in Christ as they serve at the Lord's Table.

Interest in the sacraments has grown vigorously in the last couple of decades.[7] Because we believe in the importance of the Holy Spirit's ministry through *his* means of grace, this is a good thing, despite reservations that we may have about ecumenical programs. Still, I hear many conservative Protestants who express much stronger convictions about what the sacraments are *not* than about what they are: instruments of God's grace. My hope is that these Meditations will strengthen the practice of the Lord's Supper in the churches and will help believers to enjoy the ministry of Christ at his Table. There is more to say about the ministry of the Supper than I have written. This is an introduction to the subject. If the reader is challenged to consider the riches of Christ sealed there, this book will reach its goal.

Part 1, "Foundations," is a brief theology of the Lord's Supper. That subject has been treated well by other writers. I have not tried to be exhaustive. However, I address theology in chapter 1, because the sacraments have many disputed points. They come up in the Meditations from time to time, and it is fitting to give the reader my own understanding of scriptural teaching about them. Chapter 2 is about

---

7 For example, see George Hunsinger, *The Eucharist and Ecumenism: Let Us Keep the Feast* (Cambridge: Cambridge University Press, 2008), who proposes a whole range of theses that would unify Eastern and Western Christianity around the actual presence of Christ's body and blood, "transelemented" in the Eucharist. The pull of sacramentalism is strong in our modern world. I make clear below that I understand Scripture to teach that the sacraments are effective by faith alone.

inviting believers to participate in the Table fellowship.[8] Chapter 3 sets out the basic themes of the Lord's Supper from the apostle Paul's "words of institution" in 1 Corinthians 11:23–26. Every observance of the Supper should present the themes found there. Then I elaborate on those basic themes in the Meditations that follow in part 2.

Strictly speaking, the reader may go directly to part 2. This is the meat of the book, presenting twenty-eight Meditations. Each Meditation explores the text listed beneath its title. The order follows the history of God's covenant salvation. In the old covenant, God sanctified his people and promised that he would come to them and bless them. In chapter 4, I explore some of these promises or "anticipations." The texts were chosen because they are basic to the New Testament presentations of the Last Supper—old-covenant promises of the redemption that Christ would accomplish: the Passover, covenant ratification at Sinai, the promised eschatological feast, and the suffering Servant of Isaiah 53. The message of the New Testament is that Christ has come, fulfilling the promises. The Meditations in chapter 5 examine the central facets of what God accomplished in Jesus' death and resurrection. These seven Meditations are based on New Testament texts that teach the nature of Christ's sacrifice on the cross (sacrifice, ransom, propitiation, reconciliation), accomplishing the redemption planned in eternity and promised in the Old Testament. The texts are from the Gospels and Epistles.

We live in the final era of redemptive history, the time of union with the resurrected Christ. Chapter 6 explores some of the immeasurable riches of this union. These fourteen Meditations explore the benefits of redemption applied: justification, ongoing forgiveness, sanctification, adoption, purity, fellowship in the body of Christ, reconciliation between believers, church unity, the strengthening of faith

---

8 The traditional term for what I describe in this chapter is "fencing the Table." I am perfectly happy with that expression, but I believe that "inviting" is, well, more inviting, without obscuring what Scripture requires us to say in public worship.

and repentance, and the glorious hope of resurrection life with God. Many more could have been added, especially from the Old Testament. But these will, I hope, stimulate the thinking of the minister.

I assume that, in ministering at the Lord's Table, the pastor should

1. introduce the Supper (give a Meditation), then
2. invite believers to the Table, then
3. read the words of institution of the Supper (Matthew 26:26–29; Mark 14:22–25; Luke 22:19–20; or 1 Corinthians 11:23–26), and
4. pray for God's blessing on the meal.

I will mention below that, because the Word of God is what makes the sacrament a sign, it is indispensable. A "Table Meditation" is not. The whole worship service should be kept to a reasonable length. Thus I do not assume that a Meditation must be given, or must be given every time. Nor do I wish the minister to compose two sermons for each worship service. Hence the Meditations here are suggestive and brief. They may be used either in whole or in part. However, brevity does not suggest triviality. The words with which the Supper is administered ought to set a gospel-theological framework around the sacrament. Faith, hope, and love are the goal: these come from the Spirit shining on his Word. I hope that these Meditations will stimulate thought, prayer, and joy and will lead to the development of each pastor's *own* way of addressing the congregation at the Table.

I wish to thank the Board of Trustees of Reformed Theological Seminary, who granted me a sabbatical leave in the fall semester of 2013 to complete this work. I also wish to thank my colleagues at Reformed Theological Seminary in Washington, DC—Peter Lee, Scott Redd, Geoff Sackett, and Chad Van Dixhoorn—for their encouragement, prayers, and wisdom. I am deeply grateful for mentors: John H. Gerstner, Meredith G. Kline—of blessed memory—Sinclair B.

Ferguson, and Richard B. Gaffin Jr. Each continues to teach me. And then there's my wife, Jackie. She is God's greatest gift and joy to me in this life. I thank God for every day that he gives me with her. This book is the result of her constant encouragement and perspective. She has served me in more ways than I can possibly say.

May the triune God, who has spread this joyful feast, strengthen the church as we eat and drink with Jesus Christ.

PART ONE

Foundations

CHAPTER ONE

Theology

This is a book about ministry at the Lord's Table, not a systematic theology. But, of course, everyone has a theology, and the Meditations for the Lord's Table, offered in part 2, express one too. I need to explain a number of points about the gospel, the sacraments, the covenant, and the Lord's Supper—points that I assume in what I write below. Since I mean these talks to be practically and pastorally beneficial to many, I have tried not to be too wordy. (I recognize that I raise a number of complex theological points. A full discussion is beyond the scope of this book.[1])

I write as a Reformed theologian and pastor, reading Holy Scripture in the line of John Calvin and the Reformed confessional tradition. As John Calvin wrote, "The sacraments take their virtue from the Word, when it is preached intelligibly."[2] That means that I understand the Lord's Supper as a sign and seal of our faith-union with Jesus Christ.[3] Richard B. Gaffin spells out the three aspects of union with

---

1 For excellent presentations, see Herman Bavinck, *Reformed Dogmatics*, vol. 4, *Holy Spirit, Church, and New Creation*, ed. John Bolt, trans. John Vriend (Grand Rapids: Baker Academic, 2008), ch. 9; and G. C. Berkouwer, *The Sacraments*, trans. Hugo Bekker, Studies in Dogmatics (Grand Rapids: Eerdmans, 1969). Many important questions, such as those related to ordination, are addressed in these theologies.

2 John Calvin, *Short Treatise on the Lord's Supper*, trans. J. K. S. Reid, Library of Christian Classics 22 (Philadelphia: Westminster, 1954), 161. Calvin's *Short Treatise* of 1541 is a theological gem.

3 See Calvin, *Inst.*, book 3 in its entirety and 2:1276–1428 (4/14–17). Richard B. Gaffin Jr. unfolds the relationship of Calvin's doctrine of salvation to that of the Westminster Standards in "Biblical Theology and the Westminster Standards," *Westminster Theological Journal* 65, no. 2 (2003): 165–79.

Christ in Paul's writings: predestinarian union (salvation planned in eternity), redemptive-historical union (salvation accomplished by the Son of God, once, for all time, for the entire church, in his death and resurrection), and existential union (salvation applied to the individual, in his own lifetime, by the Holy Spirit). The Meditations here are spoken to those who share this threefold union with Christ—that is, to professing believers. Let me unpack that further.

GOSPEL

As I understand the apostle Paul, the heart of the gospel is union with the once crucified, now resurrected, Jesus Christ, by faith alone.[4] Guilty and helpless in themselves, believers, by God's gracious action, nevertheless receive what is now Christ's as the result of his saving death and resurrection. In an important summary statement, Paul wrote, "Because of him you are in Christ Jesus, who became to us wisdom from God, righteousness and sanctification and redemption" (1 Cor. 1:30). It is a rich idea, as well as a beautifully simple one. When we are joined to him by faith, we receive the riches of his saving work.

Paul writes in 1 Corinthians 15:1–4 that at the center of his gospel (the things "of first importance") is Jesus Christ in his death for our sins and his resurrection on the third day, both as the necessary fulfillment of the Old Testament Scriptures. Jesus Christ and what God accomplished through his ministry, once, for all time, is the basis of salvation. Fulfilling all the promises of the biblical covenants, God established the new covenant in Jesus' blood. This is the final, superlative, and unsurpassable expression of God's covenant bond with his people.

Paul's phrase "for our sins" summarizes our need. Since birth, we have each been guilty of the transgression of God's law, of rebellion

---

4 For a thorough presentation, see Richard B. Gaffin Jr., *By Faith, Not by Sight: Paul and the Order of Salvation*, 2nd ed. (Phillipsburg, NJ: P&R Publishing, 2013), especially 40–46.

against our rightful Creator and Lord. God's righteous reaction to our sins is holy wrath. However, our guilt also entails our corruption and aversion of heart to God's holy person and his standards. Thus, as Paul puts it, we and all of humanity are completely helpless—guilty, enslaved, and perverse in our rebellion against him. Our first father, Adam, willfully put us in this position (see Rom. 5:12–21). However, God is rich in mercy, and on account of his free grace he sent his eternal Son to save us by his death and resurrection.

Whatever we needed—and we needed everything—Jesus Christ accomplished for us in these climactic events. Paul summarizes this by writing that Christ "was delivered up for our trespasses and raised for our justification" (Rom. 4:25). The Father raised him up and exalted him to his right hand in his ascension into heaven. From there Christ bestowed the Holy Spirit on the church, on the day of Pentecost, as his personal representative (Acts 2:32–33). Today the Spirit gives us life by working faith in us and so uniting us to our living head. He indwells and overcomes the resistance of rebels, sweetly drawing them to the Savior.

The term "head" brings into view that Christ is our representative before God.[5] As the "second Adam" and the "last Adam,"[6] he acted in the place of God's elect people to meet the twofold demand of the covenant broken in Adam. In our place and for us, in other words, Jesus obeyed his Father in all things and suffered death as our substitute. By this death he turned away God's righteous wrath. In Jesus' obedience, God provided an obedience that meets the demands of his law. God provided satisfaction for the righteous demand of his offended justice through Jesus' suffering and death. God then raised him bodily from the grave on the third day.[7]

---

5 Covenant theology uses the biblical term "Mediator" to summarize Christ's work in its many aspects. See 1 Timothy 2:5–6; Hebrews 9:15; 12:24.

6 See Romans 5:12–21; 1 Corinthians 15:21–22, 44–49.

7 In the words of the Westminster Shorter Catechism, this is "the redemption purchased by Christ" (question and answer 29).

Paul, in his apostolic, God-breathed proclamation, interprets Jesus' resurrection as his "redemption" from the consequences of our sins. Jesus did not, of course, need to be redeemed himself, since he had no sin (see 2 Cor. 5:21). This is what God accomplished in him *for us*. Paul uses the ideas of "justification" (e.g., Acts 26:18; Rom. 3:24, 26, 28, 30; 4:2, 5, 25), "adoption" (Rom. 8:15, 23; Gal. 4:5), and "sanctification" (Rom. 6:19, 22; 1 Cor. 1:2, 30; 6:11; Eph. 5:26) to describe the saving benefits that believers receive. These benefits belong to believers because they belong first to Christ as resurrected. Sin, alienation, and death were Christ's portion, as (and only because) he suffered "for us." But when God raised him up, he declared Jesus the "Righteous One" (Acts 22:14). In other words, God justified Christ. Unlike us, he was *not* guilty, and that is what God declared by the action of raising him from death (1 Tim. 3:16).[8] He was declared righteous by the act of resurrection.

Likewise, the Father "adopted" Christ, or, in Paul's words, declared him "Son of God in power" by his resurrection (Rom. 1:3–4). Weakness and suffering had been his experience and his burden as he came into our cursed world to save us. Glory was his as God's eternal equal. Though he was the eternal Son of God, he took on our weakness when he took our flesh in Mary's womb. That weakness, and indeed accursedness, reached its nadir in his sufferings on the cross. But God put all that behind his Son when he raised him in power. Weakness, accursedness, and death now have no power over him. Last, though he never committed sin, nor was ever inclined to do so, Jesus came under sin's domination, or power, in his death. Sin oppressed him like an evil lord. But, again, God delivered him from

---

8 The word ἐδικαιώθη (*edikaiōthei*), which the ESV text of this verse translates as "vindicated," can also be translated as "justified" (see note here in the ESV). Richard B. Gaffin Jr. argues that "justified" is the proper rendering (see his *Resurrection and Redemption: A Study in Paul's Soteriology* [1978; repr., Phillipsburg, NJ: Presbyterian and Reformed, 1987], 119–22). Jesus' resurrection as last Adam was God's effective declaration of his perfect obedience.

that power by raising him. Now sin has no power whatsoever over him (see Rom. 6:10).[9]

That is gospel good news, because when we simply trust in him, we too receive life from the dead—we are justified, adopted, and sanctified. These gifts show that as believers we are united with the resurrected Christ.[10] We have received the judicial verdict "righteous" (Christ's righteousness "counted" as ours). Every sin is forgiven. Likewise, we have been adopted into the Father's family. And we also have been freed from sin's power. Every benefit of the grace of God is found in union with the resurrected Christ. Christ is all in all. "The risen, exalted Christ is what he now is, with his benefits in their saving power."[11] God has dealt with our guilt decisively (see Rom. 4:6–8). God has removed the alienation, welcoming us forever as his children (see Gal. 3:26). We know him as our Father. God has given us new power over the remains of sin in this life (see Rom. 6:10–12). We are no longer enslaved to sin.

These riches, to be had by faith in the resurrected Christ, are, with him, the content of the Christian gospel. The Lord's Supper seals that gospel to our hearts.

SACRAMENTS

"Sacrament" is the word used by the historic church to describe circumcision, the Passover, baptism, and the Lord's Supper, "signs and seals"

---

9 Sinclair B. Ferguson develops this in *The Holy Spirit*, Contours of Christian Theology, ed. Gerald S. Bray (Downers Grove, IL: InterVarsity Press, 1996), 103–6. See also Richard B. Gaffin Jr., *Resurrection and Redemption: A Study in Paul's Soteriology* (1978; repr., Phillipsburg, NJ: Presbyterian and Reformed, 1987).

10 See Westminster Larger Catechism, question and answer 69: "What is the communion in grace which the members of the invisible church have with Christ? The communion in grace which the members of the invisible church have with Christ is their partaking of the virtue of his mediation, in their justification, adoption, and sanctification, and whatever else, in this life, manifests their union with him."

11 I am indebted to Dr. Richard B. Gaffin for this sentence, but I am unable to locate its source.

of God's gracious covenant relationship.[12] Circumcision and Passover were Old Testament rites, baptism and the Supper the continuing rites of the new covenant. God himself authored, or instituted, sacraments as instruments alongside his Word to communicate his grace to his covenant people.[13] In the view of the Protestant churches, "grace" in Scripture is not a "material something" (something "in" us[14]), but God's personal and unmerited favor, sovereignly exercised toward the guilty, transforming the whole person.[15] "I will have mercy on whom I have mercy, and I will have compassion on whom I have compassion" (Rom. 9:15). By grace, God calls us into union with Christ and, in that union, justifies and sanctifies.[16] It is pure gift; therefore, only God can show this saving grace to people, and only he can specify *how* he will do it. The Bible tells us that he does this by the Word and by sacraments.[17]

After their fall into sin, amazingly, God did not cease speaking to our first parents, Adam and Eve. Rather, he reversed their new, sinful allegiance to Satan, renewing his relationship with them, and promised them mercy in the redeeming work of Christ (Gen. 3:15). They

---

12 I refer to the historic Protestant understanding of the sacraments.

13 See Bavinck, *Reformed Dogmatics*, 4:468–82.

14 Broadly speaking, by contrast, the medieval understanding of grace was something like a substance, supernaturally poured into the soul. Roger Haight writes, "Since the time of Aquinas, the term *grace* designated primarily, although not exclusively, 'created grace,' a habit or quality of the human soul, infused by God" ("Sin and Grace," in *Systematic Theology: Roman Catholic Perspectives*, 2nd ed., ed. Francis S. Fiorenza and John P. Galvin [Minneapolis: Fortress, 2011], 404, italics his). Haight contrasts this with contemporary Roman Catholic theology since Karl Rahner, which identifies grace as God's orientation to all human beings always. Cf. *Catechism of the Catholic Church with Modifications from the Editio Typica*, 2nd ed. (New York: Doubleday, 1997), 354 (paragraph 1266), which clearly sounds the medieval note; as well as Berkouwer, *Sacraments*, 143; and Herman Bavinck, *Reformed Dogmatics*, vol. 3, *Sin and Salvation in Christ*, ed. John Bolt, trans. John Vriend (Grand Rapids: Baker Academic, 2006), 517.

15 See Bavinck, *Reformed Dogmatics*, 4:92–93.

16 Justification and sanctification are distinct benefits of union with Christ. They are distinct from each other but inseparable in the believer. See Westminster Larger Catechism, question and answer 69.

17 The whole creation bears witness to God (Rom. 1:19–21), but it does not reveal his plan of salvation. Christ's lordship does not imply that he is incarnate in all things, nor does his incarnation give saving power to the elements of creation.

believed this promise. Thus we have the first instance of saving grace, revealed and effective for sinful people. We will say more about God's covenant of grace below, but it was by his sovereign choice then, and ever since, that God communicated "the mystery of his will, according to his good pleasure" (Eph. 1:9 ASV) to save rebels and become their Friend, their Lord, their Husband, and their Father. Holy Scripture itself is the record of the developing history of God's saving acts for his people and his verbal interpretation of those acts. Think, for example, of God redeeming his people from Egypt in the exodus and the Scripture that followed, written by Moses. Every saving work that God did in history led to, and was fulfilled finally by, God's Son (see Heb. 1:1–2). For example, Christ is the heir of all God's promises to Abraham (Gal. 3:16). In 2 Corinthians 1:20, Paul writes, "For all the promises of God find their Yes in him. That is why it is through him that we utter our Amen to God for his glory." Christ, as the fulfillment of every covenant promise, is the Father's Yes. As the Head and Savior of the church, he leads the church in its "Amen."[18] Holy Scripture plays its part in God's saving activity as words of divine revelation. Through that Word, proclaimed by prophets, apostles, and now by other ministers, God reveals his will to save a people and calls them powerfully and effectively into fellowship with Christ.

To that Word of God, with all its rich contents, God has added "signs" and "seals." Many times in history God added signs to his words (e.g., the rainbow, Gen. 9:11–15; circumcision, Gen. 17:11; Jesus' miraculous multiplication of the loaves, John 6:27; and so on). Signs confirmed his promises to the faith of his people. Until Jesus returns, sacraments are the regular and permanent signs and seals of God's grace in Christ, which is continually proclaimed in his Word. When we say "sign" in reference to the sacraments, we mean, in the

---

18 I am indebted to Dr. Nelson D. Kloosterman for this sentence ("Proverbs 22:6 and Covenant Succession," in *To You and Your Children: Examining the Biblical Doctrine of Covenant Succession*, ed. Benjamin K. Wikner [Moscow, ID: Canon Press, 2005], 56).

words of Herman Bavinck, something that "images and assures us of the action of Christ."[19] So, for example, the water of baptism images the washing away of the pollution of sins by the blood and Spirit of Christ. Christ does the washing, but his action is invisible. Baptism is a "sign" of it. The believer receives it as a seal of what is "signed." Baptism seals to my faith that I have been cleansed by God.

An important point that distinguishes the Reformed tradition's understanding of the sacraments is that the biblical signs are primarily words *from* God about God's saving actions, not first about human faith, necessary as faith is. There is an inherent theological logic here, grounded in biblical religion: God sovereignly acts to save. Only then do we respond in faith. I do not deny that we confess faith as we partake,[20] but rather I deny that the sacraments are *our* word first of all. They are, first of all, God's words. The sacraments have an objective character, as the promises do.[21] The signs speak of God's grace, and faith is to be strengthened by them.

Notice Paul's description of Abraham's circumcision in Romans 4:11: "He received the sign of circumcision as a seal of the righteousness that he had by faith while he was still uncircumcised. The purpose was to make him the father of all who believe." Paul identifies circumcision as a sign and a seal of the righteousness that Abraham had by faith. Some would read Romans 4:11 as saying that it was a sign and seal of Abraham's faith. But Paul does not say that. He says it is a sign and seal of the righteousness, which is received by faith. In other words, it was a sign and seal of the righteousness that God promised to provide Abraham in his covenant (see Gen. 17:11–12). Abraham received the benefits of the salvation that would be secured by Christ, the very righteousness of God revealed in the gospel, by

---

19 Bavinck, *Reformed Dogmatics*, 4:475.

20 Clearly we do: "you proclaim the Lord's death until he comes" (1 Cor. 11:26).

21 Augustine called them "visible words" ("Tractate 80 on John 15:1–3," in *Nicene and Post-Nicene Fathers*, 1st series, vol. 7, ed. Philip Schaff [Grand Rapids: Eerdmans, 1956], 344).

faith in the promise. Circumcision was a sign and seal to him of that gift of righteousness. What about to us, who live after Christ's death and resurrection? We receive that same gift of righteousness, by faith in the promise, as it has now been fulfilled in Christ. The sign is also a seal: it confirms to the believing conscience that that righteousness belongs personally to us.

This implies that sacraments are indispensable for our faith, but only as they depend on the Word of the gospel. We must believe the gospel Word to be saved.[22] The sacraments strengthen faith that rests upon that Word.[23] It is our proneness to unbelief, even as believers, that God addresses by adding sacraments to the promises of the Bible.[24] But if they seal the biblical Word, what exactly do they say? What may amaze some of us who were not raised in a rich sacramental tradition is this: their content is the whole content of the Bible, Jesus Christ himself in every dimension of his ministry and the salvation he bestows. As Bavinck writes, "Christ—the full, rich, total Christ, both according to his divine and his human natures, with his person and work, in the state of his humiliation and in that of his exaltation—is the 'internal matter,' the 'heavenly substance,' the thing signified in the sacrament."[25]

This is why the Bible describes the benefits of the sacraments as

---

22 Bavinck writes, "Nor are they absolutely necessary for salvation, for Scripture binds salvation only to faith (John 3:16; Mark 16:16)" (*Reformed Dogmatics*, 4:489).

23 Separated from the Word, the sacraments are not indispensable. A person may be saved without baptism and the Lord's Supper, as the thief on the cross was (Luke 23:42–43), but not without faith in the gospel. That was, of course, an abnormal situation, but it nevertheless illustrates the relationship of Word and sacrament. Bavinck writes, "The sacraments do not work faith, but reinforce it, as a wedding ring reinforces love" (ibid).

24 The Belgic Confession (1561), article 33, reads: "We believe that our gracious God, taking account of our weakness and infirmities, has ordained the sacraments for us, thereby to seal unto us his promises, and to be pledges of the good will and grace of God toward us, and also to nourish and strengthen our faith; which He has joined to the word of the gospel, the better to present to our senses both that which He declares to us by His Word, and that which He works inwardly in our hearts, thereby confirming in us the salvation which he imparts to us."

25 Bavinck, *Reformed Dogmatics*, 4:477.

saving benefits: forgiveness, regeneration, sanctification, washing, and so on (see Acts 22:16; Rom. 6:3–4; 1 Cor. 10:16; and others). We may speak of the signs as though they were the saving realities, but that is the correct way to speak of them only because God has made them *signs* of those realities.[26] Where faith is present—which is to say, where a person is in Christ—the signs actually convey Christ. Here, like the promises of God, the signs "speak," providing fellowship with the living Lord (see 1 Cor. 10:16–21). So, with Calvin, I reject the idea of the sacraments as "empty signs." They are not Christ. But God communicates Christ through them, to the believer, along with the Word.[27]

In the last couple of decades, interest in the sacraments has increased among evangelical Christians. For those of us who believe in justification by faith alone, this might be a cause for concern. Should symbols take the place of the promises of God? Are more evangelicals turning from faith to ritual? No doubt some are. The turn toward the sacraments might be a turn away from the gospel of free grace in Christ, if it is unthinking. But, in Scripture, the sacraments do not communicate the grace of God apart from faith in the gospel that brings us Christ. Thus a renewed interest in the sacraments need *not* be an obscuring of the gospel. In Holy Scripture the sacraments signify and seal that union with Christ that the Spirit effects by faith. If, as the Bible presents them, God has ordained the sacraments to strengthen faith in Christ, diminishing them will impoverish faith in Christ rather than protect it.

Two more factors tie the sacraments and the Word of God together. First, like the Word, the sacraments are instruments in the

---

26 See Westminster Confession of Faith, 27.3.

27 "Unless a man means to call God a deceiver, he would never dare assert that an empty symbol is set forth by him. Therefore if the Lord truly represents the participation in his body through the breaking of bread, there ought not to be the least doubt that he truly presents and shows his body" (Calvin, *Inst.*, 2:1371 [4/17.10]). I will say more about the manner of Christ's presence below.

hand of the Holy Spirit. Neither minister nor water, bread nor wine, has the power to effect communion with God. He is the worker, the One who comes to strengthen faith through their use. The Word of God itself falls on deaf ears unless God opens our hearts, as he did Lydia's when she heard Paul's preaching (see Acts 16:14). Likewise, the sacraments are effective for faith only as the Spirit of Christ applies Christ to our hearts through them. And, since he has promised to use them, we should employ them with expectation.

Second, like the Word, only the response of (Spirit-worked) faith appropriates, or receives, Christ in the sacraments. Unless the promise of the gospel is believed, Christ remains outside us. We receive no benefit from what he has done. Note Calvin's statement at the beginning of book 3 of his *Institutes*: "First, we must understand that as long as Christ remains outside of us, and we are separated from him, all that he has suffered and done for the salvation of the human race remains useless and of no value for us."[28] Exactly the same is true of the sacraments. They emblemize the saving work of Christ and seal it when we receive them by faith. Hence, like the Word, they always call us to deeper faith in Christ. Like the gospel, the sacraments are effective by faith alone. The Spirit working with the sacramental Word strengthens faith. God works and we believe, receiving Christ.[29]

COVENANT

The cup in the Lord's Supper signifies "the new covenant in my blood" (1 Cor. 11:25). Much could be (and has been) written on the

---

28 Ibid., 1:537 (3/1.1).

29 "Therefore, I make such a division between the Spirit and the sacraments that the power to act rests with the former, and the ministry alone is left to the latter—a ministry empty and trifling, apart from the action of the Spirit, but charged with great effect when the Spirit works within, and manifests his power" (ibid., 2:1284 [4/14.9]).

subject of the covenant relation between God and his people.[30] But, as a brief summary, my understanding of the whole of biblical teaching is that "covenant" is a matter of a living relationship of mutual, voluntary commitment between God and man, created in God's image, binding each to the other. God establishes this bond sovereignly and calls upon man to respond in faith and obedience. This is momentous, of course, because the very existence of a religious bond assumes God's sovereign self-commitment. God was free *not* to bind himself to his creatures, but he chose to do it![31]

Before the fall into sin, God promised a higher life to Adam and his descendants, should Adam pass the test of obedience.[32] He failed the test of the covenant of works, rebelling against his God, and that brought the human race into bondage to sin, death, and curse (see Rom. 5:12–21), as well as bringing a curse on the whole non-image-bearing creation (Rom. 8:20–22). Nevertheless, God did not abandon his children. In place of his threatened righteous wrath, God showed mercy by reinstituting the relationship with Adam's chosen descendants (Gen. 3:15–17).[33]

But, with the fall, the situation had changed fundamentally. Man is in rebellion. In his grace, God maintains continuity in the relationship, but man now needs redemption. Thus the covenant will have to provide it, and that redemption must come about in pure sovereignty,

---

30 I am deeply indebted to Meredith G. Kline's biblical-theological exposition of the divine covenants. See his *Kingdom Prologue: Genesis Foundations for a Covenantal Worldview* (Overland Park, KS: Two Age Press, 2000). Nevertheless, I find myself in closer agreement with O. Palmer Robertson's overall presentation in *The Christ of the Covenants* (Phillipsburg, NJ: Presbyterian and Reformed, 1980), especially regarding the Mosaic covenant. Apart from Robertson's rejection of the so-called *pactum salutis* (which I do not reject), his overall presentation is quite consistent with historic Reformed theology. Cf., for example, Bavinck, *Reformed Dogmatics*, 3:193–232.

31 Just as God was free not to create the world, but he chose to do so. See Westminster Confession of Faith, 7.1.

32 See Westminster Confession of Faith, 7.2, on the "covenant of works." Bavinck argues for this understanding in *Reformed Dogmatics*, vol. 2, *God and Creation*, ed. John Bolt, trans. John Vriend (Grand Rapids: Baker Academic, 2004), 564–80.

33 See Robertson, *Christ of the Covenants*, 93–107.

apart from human contribution. Human beings are friends of Satan, not of God. They are offensive to the Holy One. Therefore, after the fall, God forges his relationship with fallen man with sacrificial blood. That blood represents both God's righteous judgment on human sin and his self-giving redemption from human sin. Palmer Robertson defines covenant as "a bond-in-blood. It involves commitments with life and death consequences."[34] Man is still God's image, though a distorted one, so he will need to be *changed* by grace if he is to believe and obey God. God both establishes the relationship and works sovereignly in the hearts of his chosen so that they are made willing and able to believe and obey.[35] In Augustine's words, he "grants what he commands."[36]

Reformed theology has called the covenant relationship, after the fall, "the covenant of grace." It is a relationship of mutual commitment between God and believing sinners, which is to say, a bond of religious fellowship initiated by God. It is not a contract but a sovereignly "imposed" relationship. For example, when God called Abram to leave his home, Genesis 12:1–3 repeats the personal pronoun "I" numerous times, indicating the Lord's direction and authority. The Lord made promises to Abram; he did not negotiate with him. There, and in all following covenant dealings, he requires a response: trusting his promises, obeying his commands, being loved and loving. Faith and obedience bring his blessing. Unbelief and disobedience bring his judgment.

Throughout Scripture the covenant relationship is expressed in the repeated summary formula, "I will be your God, and you shall be my people" (Jer. 7:23; see also Ex. 6:7; Lev. 26:12; Jer. 11:4; Rev. 21:7).

---

34 Ibid., 14.

35 See Westminster Confession of Faith, 7.3. This obedience is simply a fruit of Spirit-worked faith. It is not an instrument by which they appropriate God's promise of eternal life. Cf. Westminster Confession of Faith, 14.2.

36 Saint Augustine, *Confessions: A New Translation by Henry Chadwick*, Oxford World's Classics (New York: Oxford University Press, 1992), 10.29.

This formula captures the dynamic and gracious relationship through-out the history of salvation in the successive covenants (with Adam, Noah, Abraham, Moses, David, the prophets, and the "new covenant").

The covenants are described in Scripture as both "many" (see Eph. 2:12) and "one" (see Ps. 105:8–15, where Scripture generalizes promises made to several individuals by using the term "covenant" in the singular).[37] This indicates their rich diversity. But in their diversity they are related to one another organically. In each successive covenant, God both fulfills his previous promises and expands on them. All of them reach their final fulfillment in the new covenant established in Jesus' death and resurrection.[38]

Christ, both before and since his incarnation in history, serves as the Mediator of the covenant (1 Tim. 2:5; Heb. 9:15; 12:24). In other words, he acts for God toward us and for us toward God. Christ brings the benefits of the covenant to us as God, and he represents us before God. The "new" and final covenant was finally ratified in his sacrificial blood (Luke 22:20). This is the context of the Lord's Supper. God's people enjoy communion with him as new covenant Mediator.

Thus, despite all the variation and development in the history of redemption, there is a basic and profound unity in the religion of the Bible. Old Testament religion is the same as New Testament religion. The classic way of stating the relationship of the Old and New Testaments is that the covenants are one in "substance" but different in "administration."[39] They all administer Christ, who is their substance. All the covenants (or the one covenant of grace) have the same promises, the same Christ, and the same benefits: forgiveness and eternal

---

37 Bruce K. Waltke writes, "The psalmist's recounting of the successive covenant promises and renewals with Abraham, Isaac and Jacob (26:3–4; 28:13–15; 35:11–12) praises God for a unified covenant act. (Ps. 105:8–15; cf. Mic. 7:20) The progressive promises and renewals constitute a complete covenant commitment of grace" (*Genesis: A Commentary* [Grand Rapids: Zondervan, 2000], 246).

38 See Robertson, *Christ of the Covenants*, ch. 3, "The Unity of the Divine Covenants," and ch. 4, "The Diversity of the Divine Covenants."

39 Westminster Confession of Faith, 7.6.

life.[40] As God reveals his grace more fully in each, his people are enabled to respond to that grace more fully.

How do they differ? They differ fundamentally as promise and fulfillment. The Old Testament, in its organic development, records the promises of the covenant of grace. For example, God promised Abraham the land of Canaan in Genesis 15:18–21. That promise was fulfilled in a partial, "typical" way through the conquest of the land by Joshua. But finally, its fulfillment will be the meek inheriting the earth, as Jesus promised (Matt. 5:5), when he returns in glory (see Heb. 4:8). Paul sees that God promised Abraham that he would be heir of the *world* (Rom. 4:13). The redemption promised in the Old has been fulfilled in the New.

The New Testament proclaims the inaugurating fulfillment of those promises in the comprehensive work of Jesus Christ. An example that virtually all Christians recognize is the Old Testament sacrificial system. The blood of sacrificial animals could not actually atone for sins, but Jesus' sacrifice on the cross did (Heb. 10:4–9). All the Old Testament institutions, in their great variety,[41] called "types" or pictures, were God revealing beforehand what he would finally do in the work of his Son. In his death and resurrection, along with Pentecost, the fulfillment has begun.

This unity of covenant religion between Old and New Testaments is basic to our understanding of the Lord's Supper. Both Old and New Testaments teach us much about the riches of Jesus Christ, and both call us to fellowship with him, to faith and to obedience. The Supper seals those riches to our hearts. The benefits that make

---

40 See Calvin, *Inst.*, 1:428–64 (2/10–11).

41 See 1 Peter 1:10–12. I have in mind prophets, priests, kings, land, temple, sacrifices, feasts, the exodus event, the Paschal Lamb, and so on—God-ordained persons, actions, events, and institutions—all intended to present a picture of the work Christ would fulfill. Cf. Geerhardus Vos, *Biblical Theology: Old and New Testaments* (Grand Rapids: Eerdmans, 1948; Edinburgh: Banner of Truth, 1975), 144–48. Citations refer to the reprint edition.

up our salvation belong alike to Old and New Testament believers. Old-covenant faith and new-covenant faith bring the same salvation (see Heb. 11:1–12:2). The difference, of course, is that now Christ has come in the fullness of time and has accomplished the promised redemption in history. Since all the sacrificial types have been fulfilled, a necessary implication is that there is no longer any "ceremonial" observance in the ministry of the church. The Holy Spirit, with the Bible and sacraments as his instruments, administers union with the exalted Lord Jesus Christ.

We wait for Christ to return (1 Thess. 1:9–10). The new covenant has been inaugurated, but it has not yet been consummated. There is a judgment to come with its final rewards and final punishments. Those who use the sacraments, like those who hear the Word, are called by God to believe in Christ. Not all believe, however; not even all who profess to believe (see John 8:30–47). This fact obscures neither the truthfulness of the Word nor of the sacraments. But it does mean that some who make use of the sacraments, in unbelief, will find them functioning to bring not blessing but judgment. That is part of the "warning message" of the covenant of grace. God is very patient. But where his gospel is finally not received in faith, God's curse will follow. There will be greater judgment to those who are included in the covenant but who do not believe and repent. They have a lawful place in the administration of the covenant in history but do not partake of Christ (see Deut. 10:16; Jer. 4:4; Rom. 2:28–29; 9:6, 11–14; Phil. 3:3; Heb. 10:26–31).[42] These texts indicate that unbelief and impenitence among God's covenant people have never been acceptable to him, either in the Old or New Testaments. To put it theologically, to be a member of the covenant people, but not to be united to Christ by faith, will lead to his judgment. Most of the time,

---

42 The gift of regeneration, and the faith and repentance that flow from it, was not theirs. But we should not conclude that this was somehow acceptable to God. The unregenerate are no less guilty for their sins in the Old Testament than in the New.

this is invisible to us in the ministry of the church. The day of the Lord will reveal the truth of men's hearts. Until then we continue, in ministry as in the whole Christian life, to walk by faith, not by sight.

The "new covenant" in Scripture is inseparable from another climactic reality announced by Jesus and the apostles: the coming of the kingdom of God. That kingdom is the comprehensive fulfillment of the promises of the Old Testament (see Mark 1:15). It is God's final order for the creation. The kingdom arrived with the coming of Christ—especially his death and subsequent exaltation to God's right hand—and, as inaugurated, it will be consummated at his return in glory. It includes nothing less than the salvation of sinners and the renewal of the entire cosmos from the consequences of sin and death.[43] Jesus' meals with his disciples anticipated the final fellowship of the kingdom of God. The Last Supper was Jesus' last such meal. Paul calls the Spirit, who ministers now, "firstfruits" (Rom. 8:23) and "down payment" (2 Cor. 5:5 HCSB) of believers' final redemption. As believers are united to Christ, they enter God's kingdom and await its consummation (Col. 1:13–14). Hope of the consummated kingdom too is signified and sealed in the Lord's Supper. As we await his return in glory, we remember his saving death and feed on his body and blood.

LAST SUPPER AND LORD'S SUPPER

We have accounts of the Last Supper, at which Jesus instituted the Lord's Supper, in Matthew 26, Mark 14, and Luke 22, as well as 1 Corinthians 11. There are slight variations of wording between these

---

43 Richard B. Gaffin Jr. is the source of this sentence (lecture, Westminster Seminary, Philadelphia, PA). Geerhardus Vos summarizes Jesus' understanding of the kingdom: "To him the kingdom exists . . . where not merely God is supreme, for that is true at all times and in all circumstances, but where God supernaturally carries through his supremacy against all opposing powers and brings man to the willing recognition of the same" (*The Kingdom of God and the Church* [1903; repr. with additions and corrections, Nutley, NJ: Presbyterian and Reformed, 1972], 50).

accounts, which are somewhat difficult to harmonize.[44] These different accounts give the different authors' perspectives on Jesus' words. The healthy impulse to harmonize them arises from the conviction that each gospel along with 1 Corinthians, and all together, present the events and words truly. Because all Scripture is God breathed (2 Tim. 3:16) and thus without error, we must hold this conviction.

A couple of insights follow. In light of the inerrancy of Scripture as God breathed, we should be certain that each account preserves Jesus' words truly, though not with maximal precision.[45] God's Word is true in all it affirms, whether or not we can see its harmony at all points. God, of course, perfectly understands the harmony of what are his own accounts of the Last Supper, taking fully into account the several human authors' distinct concerns. And, as Vern Poythress writes concerning the Gospels' accounts,

> Because God is the divine author of each Gospel, each Gospel represents not only a distinct *human* perspective, but also a distinct *divine* perspective. God speaks not only what is common to the Gospels—some kind of "core"—but what is distinct in each one . . . through the Holy Spirit, he empowered them to write exactly what they wrote. All of it is God's Word.[46]

This is true, then, of the texts that speak of the Supper. Second, the multiplicity of accounts presents us with a rich and nuanced di-

---

44 Harmonization is certainly a worthy task, and in principle possible, but one I do not undertake. See I. Howard Marshall, *Last Supper and Lord's Supper* (London: Paternoster, 1980; repr. Vancouver: Regent College, 2006); and Joachim Jeremias, *The Eucharistic Words of Jesus*, trans. Norman Perrin (1977; repr., Philadelphia: Fortress, 1981) for the full discussion.

45 For a fine discussion of the relationship of Scripture's truthfulness to its precision, see John M. Frame, *The Doctrine of the Word of God*, A Theology of Lordship 4 (Phillipsburg, NJ: P&R Publishing, 2010), 167–74.

46 Vern S. Poythress, *Inerrancy and the Gospels: A God-Centered Approach to the Challenges of Harmonization* (Wheaton, IL: Crossway, 2012), 35, italics his.

vine revelation of the meaning of the Lord's Supper.[47] Working from these premises, I will seek to pay some attention to the various aspects of the presentation of the Supper in Scripture.

Jesus instituted the Lord's Supper as he ate his last Passover with the disciples.[48] His institution establishes the church's continuing understanding and mandate. God redeemed Israel from Egypt in the exodus. The first Passover sacrifice was the basis of that redemption (Ex. 12:13, 23, 27). In the Passover meal in the Old Testament, God met with his people and, on the basis of the sacrifice made and accepted (Ex. 12:27; 34:25), united himself with them in joyful celebration.[49]

Jesus' disciples dreaded his impending death. He chose the bread and wine of the Passover meal as signs of his body and blood, as they would soon be offered in sacrifice for them. By the bread and wine, he showed them that his death would bring about the forgiveness of the new covenant that was pictured and foretold in the Old Testament.

Jesus' sacrificial death fulfilled the Passover (and much besides) as the reality promised by the Old Testament symbols. Jesus' death was the substance of all the sacrifices of the Old Testament, which promised and prefigured it: the "sacrifice" of Isaac (Gen. 22), the Passover lamb (Ex. 12:26–27; 1 Cor. 5:6–8; 1 Peter 1:18–19), the blood of the covenant at Sinai (Ex. 24:8; Matt. 26:27–28), the suffering of the

---

47 Bavinck writes, "The variant readings sufficiently demonstrate that Jesus no more prescribed a fixed and unchangeable formula at the Supper than he did in connection with baptism. It is even impossible to determine the literal words employed by Jesus on this occasion. He did not define exactly what had to be said at the Supper, but he described what it was and had to be" (*Reformed Dogmatics*, 4:547). This also entails, of course, the conclusion that Jesus' words were not a "consecration" formula.

48 Commentators debate this, but the conclusion remains sound. For example, Robert Letham disputes Passover as the occasion (*The Lord's Supper: Eternal Word in Broken Bread* [Phillipsburg, NJ: P&R Publishing, 2001], 4–5). For the arguments in its favor, see Jeremias, *Eucharistic Words*, 41–88; and Marshall, *Last Supper*, 57–80.

49 See Bavinck, *Reformed Dogmatics*, 4:542–43.

Servant of the Lord (Isa. 53:12; Matt. 26:28).[50] In Jeremiah 31:31 the Lord had promised to make a new covenant with his people. Jesus told the disciples that his blood is the true sacrifice that would effect that covenant (Luke 22:20) and bring about a new exodus of salvation for the church.

Let me say here that the Last Supper was not *itself* Jesus' sacrifice, and neither is the Lord's Supper a sacrifice.[51] It is served not on an altar but on a table.

The Passover lamb was sacrificed not at the Passover meal but before the meal. Jesus was sacrificed not at the meal but after the meal. So the Supper is a meal of fellowship with God on the *basis* of Jesus' historic sacrifice. In the Lord's Supper, the sacrifice, offered once for all time, is the presupposition, not the content, of the meal. The Last Supper sealed Jesus' sacrifice, *about to be offered* on the cross, to the twelve. Theological controversy must not blind us to the very obvious fact that Jesus spoke the words "This is my body" (Matt. 26:26–27; Mark 14:22, 24; Luke 22:19–20), and so on, to the *disciples*, not "to" the elements.[52] He spoke to the Twelve, building their faith, sealing what he was about to do on Calvary. The Lord's Supper seals the sacrifice, once offered on the cross, to believers. The Supper is the meal of the fellowship of blessing with God, achieved by Jesus' blood shedding. Its focus is not "elements" of bread and wine, but Jesus' death for us, which they show.

The characteristic pairing of words in Jesus' statements supports this position. Jesus called the bread and wine "my body" (Luke 22:19) and "my blood" (Matt. 26:28; Mark 14:24). This pairing of σῶμα

---

50 See Herman Ridderbos, *The Coming of the Kingdom*, trans. H. de Jongste (Philadelphia: Presbyterian and Reformed, 1962), 425. Christ is our Passover lamb (1 Cor. 5:7). But it was not the Passover sacrifice, as such, to which he referred in his words about the bread. He distributed not the roast lamb, but bread, to represent his body given.

51 This is the unanimous testimony of the Reformed Confessions.

52 In other words, there is no notion in Scripture of a word of consecration that transforms bread and wine. See Bavinck, *Reformed Dogmatics*, 4:463.

(*sōma*, "body") and αἷμα (*haíma*, "blood") should not be abstracted from their significance in covenant history, as undue stress on the idea of "elements" tends to do. The words signified death. Herman Ridderbos pinpoints their sense:

> Body and blood undoubtedly occur here as the two compo-
> nents of man's material make-up which are separated at *death*.
> And it is death that is meant here. For Jesus' body is mentioned
> here as that which "is given for you" (Luke), and his blood as
> that which "is shed for many for the remission of their sins"
> (Matt. and Mark). Both this "given" and this "shed" refer to
> Jesus' impending death.[53]

Jeremias comments, "Each of the two nouns presupposes a slay-ing that has separated flesh and blood."[54] Scripture frequently speaks of Jesus' death on the cross using the word "give/gave/given," refer-ring to Jesus' self-offering, as in Mark 10:45; Galatians 1:4; 1 Timo-thy 2:6; and Titus 2:14.

More specifically, when Jesus said, "This is my body," he referred not to what he was *breaking*, but to what he was *distributing*.[55] Jesus' action of breaking the bread in no way suggested the violent tearing asunder of his body.[56] Rather, it was the customary action of the father

---

53 Ridderbos, *Coming of the Kingdom*, 424, italics his.

54 Jeremias, *Eucharistic Words*, 222. Thus, though Jesus' words about the bread and his words about the cup were separated by the meal, they did not refer to different reali-ties, such as Jesus' presence (bread) and sacrifice (cup). They referred together to the sacrifice.

55 In Luke 22:19, "had given thanks" and "broke" and "gave" precede the "saying."

56 Marshall writes, "'Breaking' is not an appropriate metaphor for killing, and the breaking of the bread is simply the preliminary to its distribution" (*Last Supper*, 86). In Luke 22:19, the present participle διδόμενον (*didómenon*, "given") has a future sense, referring to Jesus' imminent death. Compare the present participles ἐκχυννόμενον (*enchunnómenon*, "is poured out") and παραδιδόντος (*paradidóntos*, "betrays") in verses 20 and 21, which similarly refer to the immediate future.

of a family as he distributed bread at every meal.[57] Likewise, his statement "This cup . . . is the new covenant in my blood" (Luke 22:20),
referred not to the action of pouring wine into the cup, but to the
wine already poured into the cup. Jesus' phrase τὸ ὑπὲρ ὑμῶν ἐκχυννόμενον (to hyper humōn enchunnómenon), "poured out for you"
(Luke 22:20), almost certainly refers to the blood shedding that would
occur in just a few hours, not to the pouring of the wine. We may see
this more clearly by noticing that the parallel passages (Matt. 26:28;
Mark 14:24) have "for many" in place of "for you."[58] Reading the texts
together, the variation from "for you" to "for many" signals that the
recipients of the "pouring out" are a group much wider than the disciples present at the Last Supper ("you"). They are all those for whom
his blood would be shed, the whole church throughout the ages. Jesus'
words in Matthew 26:28 strengthen this conclusion: "my blood of the
covenant, which is poured out for many for the forgiveness of sins."

---

57 Most of us are familiar with the King James rendering of 1 Corinthians 11:24, which
reads, "broken for you." We should note, however, that the word κλωμενον (klōme-
non, "broken") is not found in the best manuscript witnesses. It is almost certainly
a scribal addition. See Bruce M. Metzger, A Textual Commentary on the Greek New
Testament (New York: United Bible Societies, 1975) ad loc, "derived from the preceding
ἔκλασεν." The language of "breaking" does not describe the performing of sacrifices
in the Old Testament. Further, if John 19:36 refers to the Passover lamb, "these things
took place that the Scriptures might be fulfilled: 'Not one of his bones will be broken,'"
the idea of "breaking" the bread as referring to sacrificing Jesus' body would be ruled
out. Commentators differ widely over the Scripture to which John alludes in verse 36.

58 Herman N. Ridderbos writes, "When Jesus says 'for this is my blood of the new covenant which is shed for many,' it cannot refer to the action of pouring wine into the cup,
but only to the distributing of the wine as the blood of Christ. And this for the simple
reason that the pouring of the wine into the cup cannot possibly be linguistically de-
noted as a 'shedding' (ekkein). When Van der Leeuw writes that Jesus 'poured out' the
wine as the blood of his new covenant and infers that in essence he was sacrificing himself at this meal, he only transfers his own ideas into the original text, and that in a very
radical way. There is not the faintest suggestion in the text of a symbolic 'pouring out'
of the wine into the cup. The parallelism between pouring out of wine and shedding
of blood is perfectly alien to the text and to linguistic usage. Besides, from the Passover
ritual, it may be inferred that the wine had been standing ready when Jesus applied the
figure of his blood to it. What is symbolized, therefore, is not Christ's self-surrender,
but its fruits for the life of his followers. Not the altar, but the table, characterizes the
activity at the Lord's Supper. The sacrifice is the presupposition preceding this eating
and drinking" (Coming of the Kingdom, 429–30, italics his). The "sacramental action"
regarding the cup is not "pouring" any more than it is "shedding."

The referent of the "pouring out," providing the basis of "the forgiveness of sins," can be no other than Jesus' blood shedding on the cross.

Thus there is almost certainly no symbolic meaning intended for our "pouring" wine into a cup. The Lord's Supper is not a sacrificial ritual, because the Last Supper was not one. When we obey his command, "Do this . . . ," we do not reenact a sacrifice.

There has been, of course, controversy for centuries about what Jesus was distributing in the Last Supper. The teaching of the Roman Catholic Church (called "transubstantiation") is that it became truly Jesus' flesh and blood, though it continued to appear as bread and wine.[59] There is no evidence for that doctrine in the gospel accounts. Such a theological reading of the Lord's Supper is, in fact, deeply unbiblical. It obscures the meaning of the Supper by focusing the attention of believers on the elements instead of on the significance of his unique death and their union with him. The Christ who was crucified for us has now been "crowned with glory and honor because of the suffering of death" (Heb. 2:9). God has glorified him, as the reward of his completed suffering, once for all (see Heb. 7:27; 9:25–28; 10:10).[60] His suffering fully satisfied the requirements of God's justice for his people. The glorified Christ is not, and cannot be again, subject to humiliation, suffering, or sacrifice.[61]

Why then did Jesus command the disciples to eat and drink, and

---

59 See *Catechism of the Catholic Church*, 383–85 (paragraphs 1373–77). This post–Vatican II document appeals also to the deliverances of the Council of Trent, which remain authoritative for Rome.

60 See also Herman Bavinck's thorough and devastating critique of the doctrine of transubstantiation in *Reformed Dogmatics*, 4:568–74. We may well ask what benefit the actual ingestion of Jesus' flesh and blood would bring us. Otfried Hofius writes, "Just as the cup or its contents *is not* the New Covenant in the sense of substance, neither is the bread in a substantial sense the body of Christ" ("The Lord's Supper and the Lord's Supper Tradition: Reflections on 1 Corinthians 11:23b–25," in *One Loaf, One Cup: Ecumenical Studies of 1 Cor 11 and Other Eucharistic Texts*, ed. Ben F. Meyer [Macon, GA: Mercer University Press, 1993], 100, italics his).

61 Calvin's point that Christ's true human body is subject to spatial limits—that he, as a human being, remains at God's right hand—is as telling today as it was in the sixteenth century (*Inst.*, 2:1372–73 [4/17.12]).

to do so repeatedly? So that they might have the assurance of sins forgiven. The bread taken and eaten, the wine drunk, represent the application of salvation to believers, because Christ's words gave them and continue to give them that meaning. As believers receive them, they receive the salvation accomplished by his death.

The writing of the apostle Paul, as the earliest "commentator" on the Last Supper (1 Cor. 11:17–34), supports these conclusions. The Supper is a sacrificial meal, in which believers appropriate the benefits of the sacrifice by eating and drinking. Paul shows that this is his own understanding in a number of ways. He repeats the words of institution. He refers to the night in which Jesus was "delivered up" [62] (a solemnizing detail indicating that Jesus' death was the fulfillment of God's plan). He makes a direct connection in verses 26–27 between the bread and cup and "the Lord's death."

Ridderbos shows the importance of Paul's teaching in the previous chapter (1 Cor. 10:1–22) for the interpretation of chapter 11. Eating sacrifices at pagan temples is participation in a sacrificial meal, which indicates fellowship with demons. Drinking and eating are a "participation" in the body and blood of Christ at the Lord's Table (1 Cor. 10:16); "the cup of blessing that we bless" and "the bread that we break"—each is a κοινωνία (koinōnía). Surely, then, the Corinthians may not "be participants" also with demons (v. 20, κοινων-ούς, koinōnous, from the same root). To eat sacrifices at the demons' table is to "participate" with them, as Israel does with the Lord when it eats the sacrificial meal (v. 18 uses the same noun, κοινωνοὶ, koinōnoi). In each case there is fellowship with the host of the meal by eating what has lain on the altar.

This helps us to see that the presence of Christ at the Lord's Table is not found in "elements," which, as Calvin would say, "bring him

---

down" to us. Instead, Christ, as Lord at the Table, makes believers share in the benefits of his sacrificial death. There is a proper distinction between Jesus' crucifixion and the atonement that God accomplished by it. It was not merely the events of those hours, but what God transacted in his plan of salvation through them, that is important for us. God interprets those events in Holy Scripture. The atonement means reconciliation *with God*, ransom paid *to God*, the propitiation *of God*, and so on. In the Supper, he makes us companions at his Table, meeting us as our reconciled God.

First Corinthians 10 helps us here as well. In verses 1–13, Paul compares the church to Israel in the wilderness. There is a covenant-historical analogy between Israel and the church. Paul identifies Israel as "our fathers" to the (Gentile) Corinthians in verse 1. What happened to them "typically" (τύποι, *tupoi*, v. 6) is a warning "for us" (v. 6), "for our instruction, on whom the end of the ages has come" (v. 11). Israel committed idolatry, despite their privileges. "Most" (v. 5, or "some," vv. 7–10) fell under God's judgment. The Corinthian church must not follow their example (v. 7). In fact, the fathers' overthrow in the wilderness is the basis of Paul's warning, later in the chapter, against committing idolatry: "Therefore, my beloved, flee from idolatry" (v. 14). This they must do rather than provoke Christ by sharing the table of demons (vv. 21–22) while seeking at the same time to participate in the Lord's Table (v. 16).

How does this bear on the Lord's Supper? In 10:1–5, Paul compares the privileges of Israel to those of the church. In doing so, he uses the language of the New Testament sacraments to describe God's blessing on Israel. Israel was redeemed from Egypt by the glory-cloud presence of the Lord. Paul calls this being "baptized into Moses" (v. 2), the covenant mediator. Likewise, Israel partook of what the apostle calls "spiritual food" and "spiritual drink" (vv. 3–4). This language appears to be borrowed from the terminology of the

Supper.[63] In the original Greek, Paul sets the two clauses in parallel and repeats the first five words in each clause; this highlights his emphasis.[64] This eating and drinking was the privilege of all the Israelites. The food and drink refer to the manna on which Israel lived (Ex. 16; Ps. 78:23–29) and the water that flowed from the rock to save them from thirst (Ex. 17:1–7; Num. 20:2–13). Their Redeemer sustained them.

But the use of the adjective πνευματικὸν (*pneumatikón*, "spiritual") in verses 3–4 for both the food and the drink that sustained Israel is most instructive. It appears to be a reference to the Holy Spirit. This is consistent with Paul's regular use of the adjective in this letter, and virtually uniformly elsewhere, as a reference to the activity of the Holy Spirit (see 2:13, 15; 3:1; 9:11; 12:1; 14:1, 37; 15:44, 46).[65] Nothing in the context suggests another meaning.[66] Manna and water were miraculous and of the Holy Spirit.[67]

Paul is saying that Israel had an experience of the presence of the preincarnate Christ and his Spirit during the wilderness period (see

---

63 So ibid., 419; and Gordon D. Fee, *The First Epistle to the Corinthians* (Grand Rapids: Eerdmans, 1987), 447.

64 See Roy E. Ciampa and Brian S. Rosner, *The First Letter to the Corinthians*, The Pillar New Testament Commentary, ed. D. A. Carson (Grand Rapids: Eerdmans, 2010), 448. They note that Paul is almost certainly not warning the Corinthians against a superstitious trust in the sacraments. He is warning against idolatry.

65 See also Romans 1:11; Ephesians 1:3; Colossians 1:9. The only exception appears to be Ephesians 6:12.

66 See Richard B. Gaffin Jr., "Life-Giving Spirit: Probing the Center of Paul's Pneumatology," *Journal of the Evangelical Theological Society* 41, no. 4 (December 1998): 573–98; and his "The Last Adam, the Life-Giving Spirit," in *The Forgotten Christ: Exploring the Majesty and Mystery of God Incarnate*, ed. Stephen Clark (Nottingham, UK: Inter-Varsity Press, 2007), 191–231.

67 Anthony C. Thiselton writes, "In its OT context, 'spiritual' food denotes *manna* provided by God as a miracle, while in the NT πνευματικὸς and especially in Paul denotes that which is of God's Spirit" (*The First Epistle to the Corinthians: A Commentary on the Greek Text*, The New International Greek Testament Commentary, ed. I. Howard Marshall and Donald A. Hagner [Grand Rapids: Eerdmans, 2000], 726, italics his). We should probably capitalize the adjective "Spiritual" in verses 3–4. See also the reference to the instruction of the Spirit, in connection with the manna and water, in Nehemiah 9:20.

v. 9, "We must not put Christ to the test, as some of them did").[68] (Paul assumes here what the historic church formulated as the doctrine of the Holy Trinity. Each of the divine persons is eternal, and each has been involved in all of God's acts in the creation. This is especially clear in the history of redemption.) Christ provided them with Spiritual food and drink.[69] He supplied their need. The water and manna functioned for them as means of grace intended to teach them their dependence on God's word of provision: "And he humbled you and let you hunger and fed you with manna, which you did not know, nor did your fathers know, that he might make you know that man does not live by bread alone, but man lives by every word that comes from the mouth of the LORD" (Deut. 8:3).[70]

Christ, by the Spirit, provided for them supernaturally. The eating and drinking were to be an exercise of faith in God's provision. However, Paul also says that some committed idolatry and fell under judgment in the wilderness (1 Cor. 10:6–10). He warns the church not to do likewise, on this covenant-historical basis ("therefore, my beloved," v. 14), by eating and drinking at idols' tables (vv. 14–22), among other sins.

This tells us, new-covenant believers, those "on whom the end of the ages has come" (v. 11), what it means to eat and drink at the Lord's Table. Our Lord provides food for us. He sustains us in a wilderness

---

68 Gordon D. Fee writes, "The same Christ who now supplies the Corinthians with the Spirit, and whom they are testing, by going to pagan feasts, had already experienced such 'testing' by Israel; and the Israelites had been overthrown in the desert. . . . It is precisely the presence of *Christ* in Israel's story that will make all of this work as a warning to the Corinthians." *Pauline Christology: An Exegetical-Theological Study* (Peabody, MA: Hendrickson, 2007), 94, italics his.

69 This is true however we are to understand the Rock's "following" them (1 Cor. 10:4).

70 Deuteronomy 8:15 refers as well to the water from the rock. Nehemiah recounts the same period in Israel's life (Neh. 9:15–21), including God's sustaining provision of manna and water and referring to Israel's rebellion, and says in verse 20, "You gave your good Spirit to instruct them and did not withhold your manna from their mouth and gave them water for their thirst."

of temptation by feeding us.[71] He is present with us and builds our faith by the work of his Spirit as we eat and drink. Although in verses 3–4 the reference is to the preincarnate Christ, for us who live after his incarnation, exaltation, and Pentecost, the Spirit grants us life-giving fellowship with the ascended Christ, at the Table, as he now is, *for us*. We receive him.[72]

Ridderbos summarizes,

> This redemptive-historical analogy also casts clear light on the New Testament Supper. As Israel was in Moses once led out of Egypt and further kept alive in the wilderness by God's miraculous power, so for the church not only does its once-for-all deliverance lie in Christ's death, but its continual food and drink as well. The Lord's Supper, as communion in the body and blood of Christ delivered up in death, is also spiritual food and drink. The sacrificial gift becomes sacrificial food, the receiving of bread and wine from the hand of the Lord, in liberation and rejoicing. Therefore, this food and drink may also be called "spiritual," pneumatic, not only because it is from heaven, but because it makes us live out of Christ's self-surrender, and thus imparts his Spirit (Rom. 5:5).[73]

SACRAMENTAL UNION

From what I have written above, it should be clear that I believe the Lord's Supper is more than a meal of memorial. It is real fellowship

---

71 I will discuss the connection between Christ as the true manna (John 6:35–58) and the "Spirit who gives life" (vv. 62–63) below. However, I believe the subject of Jesus' discourse is not the Supper but what the Supper represents—union with him where he now is, in heaven.

72 Paul identifies the work of the ascended, glorified Christ in the church with the work of the Spirit (Rom. 8:9–10; 1 Cor. 3:17–18; Eph. 3:16–17). Cf. Gaffin's presentation in "Life-Giving Spirit," 583–84.

73 Ridderbos, *Paul*, 420.

with the resurrected Christ by means of the action of his Spirit. There is no sacrifice made, but the whole outward transaction of the meal, including eating and drinking bread and wine, are, for believers, real fellowship with the Lord. There is little doubt in my mind about that, based on Paul's questions in 1 Corinthians 10:16: "The cup of blessing that we bless, is it not a participation in the blood of Christ? The bread that we break, is it not a participation in the body of Christ?" These questions carry their answers within them. Paul uses the word κοινωνία (*koinōnía*) twice, meaning real fellowship with Christ, who was sacrificed for us (cf. v. 18, referring to the sacrifice on Israel's altar). While it certainly includes "remembrance," this is more than an act of the mind or intellect.[74] Eating the bread and drinking the cup are receiving anew the sustenance that comes from the sacrifice of the Lord.

Jesus commanded the disciples to eat and drink, and to do so repeatedly; Paul repeats ὁσάκις (*hosákis*), "as often as," in 1 Cor. 11:25–26.[75] We receive the bread and cup as receiving him. Communion with Christ comes about by the work of the Holy Spirit as we eat and drink, believing. Eating the bread thus is taking Christ into our hearts anew. Drinking the cup thus is receiving Christ's blood. This happens not physically or locally, but through the ministry of the Spirit. What we see are the signs; what we have is the reality.[76] The sign and the reality are described in terms that reflect each other. This

---

74 I will address the meaning of "remembrance" below.

75 Commenting on Luke 22:19, David G. Peterson writes, "The present tense of the Greek imperative implies the need to go on doing what Jesus commands: eating and drinking in remembrance of him" (*Encountering God Together: Leading Worship Services That Honor God, Minister to His People, and Build His Church* [Phillipsburg, NJ: P&R Publishing, 2013], 167).

76 See Calvin's comment on "this is my body": "This expression is a metonymy, a figure of speech commonly used in Scripture when mysteries are under discussion. . . . Though the symbol differs in essence from the thing signified (in that the latter is spiritual and heavenly, while the former is physical and visible), still, because it not only symbolizes the thing that it has been consecrated to represent as a bare and empty token, but also truly exhibits it, why may its name not rightly belong to the thing?" (*Inst.*, 2:1305 [4/17.21]).

is the "sacramental union" supported by the Scriptures.

The Reformed confessions use vigorous language to describe the presence of Christ in the Supper. For example, the Belgic Confession, article 35, says,

> Though Christ always sits at the right hand of his Father in the heavens, yet does he not therefore cease to make us partakers of himself by faith. This feast is a spiritual table, at which Christ communicates himself with all his benefits to us, and gives us there to enjoy both himself and the merits of his sufferings and death: nourishing, strengthening, and comforting our poor comfortless souls, by the eating of his flesh, quickening and refreshing them by their drinking of his blood.

However, the confessions qualify carefully, so as to deny a physical presence or one that would identify Christ's actual body and blood with the elements.[77] "It is receiving from his hands and eating and drinking of the fruits of his cross until he comes to drink the new wine with his followers in his Father's Kingdom."[78] This has been the Reformed understanding of Holy Scripture, and I follow it here. "All, like hungry men, should flock to such a bounteous repast."[79]

---

77 See Heidelberg Catechism, question and answer 78, 80; Westminster Confession of Faith, 29.6–7. Cf. Cornelis P. Venema, "The Doctrine of the Lord's Supper in the Reformed Confessions" *Mid-America Journal of Theology* 12 (2001): 135–99.
78 Ridderbos, *Coming of the Kingdom*, 439.
79 Calvin, *Inst.*, 2:1424 (4/17.46).

CHAPTER TWO

Inviting

In the whole of Jesus' public ministry, he showed God's grace toward unworthy people. He welcomed people who were otherwise socially or morally unacceptable to table fellowship. He called them to partake with him in the future messianic banquet promised by the prophets (see Luke 13:24–30; 14:15–24; and so on). He turned no one away who was willing to hear his teaching, but invited all to faith and repentance. Many did believe, and many did not.

The Last Supper was Jesus' final meal before his suffering. It too anticipated the messianic banquet. There Jesus invited his disciples to share the fellowship of the new covenant with him. He was soon to offer himself on the cross as the final sacrifice for sin. The Lord's Supper carries on the meaning of the Last Supper. Because Jesus marked *this* bread and wine as a seal of his saving death (and of the new covenant), the fellowship it marks is closer than that of the other meals in the Gospels. Those meals welcomed people who were "in transition" into the kingdom. But, unlike the bread and wine of the Lord's Supper, Jesus did not make the food a sign of participation in his saving death. Jesus' sacrifice on the cross is the basis of saving fellowship with God, the fellowship of faith and repentance. This meal signifies participation in saving grace. He commanded that the meal be observed in his church until he returns.

The pastor invites the church to partake of the Supper. He invites Jesus' disciples to share fellowship at the Table with Jesus and his family. The invitation to the Table, then, is made to believers. It is not a general offer of the bread and wine to everyone in the congregation. Instead, it is an invitation to those who believe to enjoy the fellowship of the church with the Lord. Since it is a communion with Christ, this feast is for those who are in union with Christ.

God gives communion with Christ in the covenant bond that he establishes with believers. God welcomes into his fellowship all who receive Christ as the only Savior. He counts them righteous and forgiven. He commits himself to continue the powerful work of new life in them by his Spirit and to care for all their needs as heavenly Father. All this is what Christ purchased for us by giving himself in our place. The Spirit of God brings us into this communion with him by giving us faith in Christ. When we feast, we enjoy communion with Christ, and that communion is founded on union with him.

One of the requirements of the covenant is that we receive water baptism in the name of the Trinity (Matt. 28:19). In baptism, God places his name on us and gives us the pledge of these gifts. Baptism seals our union with Jesus Christ. Accordingly, only baptized believers should be invited to the Lord's Table.[1]

Further, new life in fellowship with God is also life in relationship with his church. We promise to serve Christ and to live lives reconciled with our brothers and sisters in Christ. By his grace, we seek to forgive each other as God has forgiven us and to love each other as Christ has loved us. We are to submit ourselves to the wholesome nurture of the elders (or otherwise designated leaders), who serve in Christ's name.[2]

---

1 God commanded Israel to admit only circumcised persons to the Passover, the old-covenant fellowship meal: "no uncircumcised person shall eat of it" (Ex. 12:48). Because the Lord's Supper is the corresponding new-covenant fellowship meal, it is rightly implied that the sign of baptism, which corresponds to circumcision, is likewise required of participants. Another way of saying this is that the Supper is for the church.

2 One NT evidence is that the apostle expected this of every believer in Thessalonica: "We ask you, brothers, to respect those who labor among you and are over you in the Lord and admonish you, and to esteem them very highly in love because of their work. Be at peace among yourselves" (1 Thess. 5:12–13).

All this is entailed in union with Christ and with his body. The invitation to the Lord's Supper, then, is to be made to baptized believers living in a reconciled relationship with Christ and his church. The phrase used in Presbyterian churches is "communicant members in good standing." "Good standing" means those whose lives are free from overt sin, the kind of sin that requires the church to exclude them.[3]

Though some would disagree, I believe we should not limit this invitation to the members of our own church. Instead, we invite all who are baptized believers, members of Jesus' church in every place, to share the fellowship of the Lord's Table. We extend the invitation this way because we wish to uphold the unity, and recognize the holiness, of the church worldwide.[4]

This is a warm invitation, but it is not indiscriminate. Some may ask whether the invitation should be so limited. Isn't faith alone the requirement for receiving the meal? Why not invite all believers? Faith unites us to Christ; this is true. But it is the *profession* of faith that unites us to the church. Remember that, although he loves them dearly, the minister is not simply expressing his feeling for the people. He is speaking on behalf of the Lord Jesus Christ. Second, we must distinguish between the Lord's Supper and a broadly religious event like a concert or a pageant. In this respect the Supper is not even like listening to gospel preaching or prayer. The gospel is for all. All are invited to receive Christ as he is offered in the gospel. God the Father calls through the Word, "Come into fellowship with my Son."

---

3 Since God has not given the elders (or other leaders) of the church the ability "mystically" to examine the heart, they can examine only a person's profession of faith, along with his behavior. Overt sin that calls a person's faith into question, or which may lead others to feel free to commit the same sin, is what Paul warned the Corinthians not to allow when he wrote, "Do you not know that a little leaven leavens the whole lump?" (1 Cor. 5:6). He goes on in the passage to urge them to exercise discipline toward a publicly sinning and unrepentant person (vv. 9–13).

4 Our congregation is not the only assembly of believers who worships Christ. We are not to act as though we thought it were.

Many believe. As Paul wrote to the Romans, "With the heart one believes and is justified, and with the mouth one confesses and is saved" (Rom. 10:10). Those who believe are then to (verbally) confess Jesus' lordship.

The Supper requires more than heart belief (though certainly not less). It is those who confess with the mouth who are to be admitted to the Table. Why? Because eating and drinking are acts that express faith. Paul wrote to the Corinthian church, "As often as you eat this bread and drink the cup, you *proclaim* the Lord's death until he comes" (1 Cor. 11:26). Those who feast are required to believe in Christ. Therefore the Lord's Supper makes a distinction in the congregation between those who believe and others who are rightly present in worship but who do not (yet) believe in Christ. It draws a line. To put it another way, God's grace is free and welcoming, but the benefits of Christ and his cross belong only to believers. The Supper is a sign of those benefits, so it is visible, and the "line" it draws is visible. This may feel wrong or even be off-putting to some, but there is no way around it if we are to proceed scripturally.[5] Still, this "line" need not, nor should it be, exaggerated by the way the pastor makes the invitation. After all, he should invite all present to believe in Christ, who freely gives his riches to all who call on him (see Rom. 10:12–13).

The apostle warned the Corinthian church not to eat and drink unworthily. That warning also applies to us. However, in the first of these invitations, I have implied it rather than stated it explicitly. I do not believe that the emphasis of the invitation should be on the danger of the Supper. It is a feast of joy, a "table of thanksgiving."

Of course, it is certainly appropriate to warn explicitly, depend-

---

5 Westminster Confession of Faith, 27.1, says that one purpose of the sacrament is to distinguish the church from the world. This is a healthy spiritual function of the Lord's Supper.

ing on the circumstances of the particular congregation to whom the minister speaks.[6] After the invitations, I have added a warning.

In my youth, ministers would sometimes urge communicant members *not* to partake if they had unconfessed sins or had broken relationships in the church. Matthew 5:23–24 was quoted as support for this:

> So if you are offering your gift at the altar and there remember that your brother has something against you, leave your gift there before the altar and go. First be reconciled to your brother, and then come and offer your gift.

However, in this passage, Jesus refers to the altar in the Jerusalem temple, not to the Lord's Table (which is emphatically *not* an altar!). Jesus requires reconciled relationships within the church. But he does not refer here to the Lord's Supper. What is more, Scripture never instructs believers *not* to partake. Rather, Paul urges persons to partake as having examined themselves: "Let a person examine himself, then, and so eat of the bread and drink of the cup" (1 Cor. 11:28). Paul says, "so eat," (οὕτως, *houtōs*, "thus"), not "so do not eat"! Finally, Table fellowship is rightly more than an individual matter. As church officers have the authority to admit a person to Communion, so, on proper grounds, they may exclude him or her. But individual members do not have the right to put themselves out of Communion. Sins unconfessed should be confessed, and relationships reconciled, but these are not, strictly speaking, prerequisites for eating and drinking. They are postrequisites. We ought certainly to

---

6 The lengthy warning section found in 1 Corinthians 11:27–34 shows how Paul corrected abuses of the Lord's Supper. The same Christ who judged Israel (1 Cor. 10:8–10) is Lord of the church. His new-covenant meal entails the possibility of both blessing and judgment.

confess our sins to God immediately, and we must also purpose, before God, to take the necessary steps to achieve reconciliation. Under these circumstances the Table will be God's means to strengthen us to do his will.

Here, then, are a number of Invitations to the Lord's Table for use by the pastor.

INVITATION ONE

On Christ's behalf I invite you to come to this Table and receive the body and blood of Christ. Come as one who has received the sign of the covenant in baptism. Come in the fellowship of God's church—either this church or another church—as you trust Christ as the Redeemer from sin, then come and receive these signs of his sacrifice. Share his fellowship as you eat and drink. Come with a heart that gives up your sins, and as a person committed to living in love with all people. If you have not come to the place where you believe in Christ—if, for example, you are still reflecting on Christ and his claims—I invite you not to the Table today, but to come to Christ *himself*. He said, "If anyone thirsts, let him come to me and drink" (John 7:37). He will give you his Spirit and welcome you to God's fellowship. When you are ready, make your faith known and be welcomed to this Table with the church.

To you who believe: come because Christ commands— not because you are worthy, nor because you are faithful, nor because you are righteous. Come because a loving Savior calls you here to nourish your faith. The apostle wrote, "For I received from the Lord what I also delivered to you, that the Lord Jesus on the night when he was betrayed took bread . . ." (1 Cor. 11:23–26).

INVITATION TWO

Jesus often welcomed "sinners" to eat with him. It was shocking to religious people how friendly he was to the unholy. Sinners loved him because he welcomed them. But when Jesus established the Lord's Supper, he sat down with his disciples. Who are disciples? People who have committed themselves to his lordship. Jesus is their Lord, and they follow his commands. Disciples find themselves, sometimes in a very mysterious way, *bound* to obey Jesus. Why? Not because they are good—they are not good, they are very needy—but because he redeemed them; he shed his blood for them.

On behalf of the elders, then, and on behalf of Jesus Christ, I invite you to receive these signs of Jesus' body and blood. Every baptized disciple of Jesus who is living in peace, reconciled with his neighbor and with the church, should come to this Table.

If you do not believe in Christ, let me ask you to consider, why not? He is trustworthy. His sacrifice was more than enough to satisfy God's requirements of you. God accepted the sacrifice of his Son on the cross and raised him from the dead. Put your trust in Christ. He will never fail you. When you do, make your faith public, so that we may share your joy and you may be welcomed to the Table of the Lord. The apostle wrote, "For I received from the Lord what I also delivered to you, that the Lord Jesus on the night when he was betrayed took bread . . ." (1 Cor. 11:23–26).

INVITATION THREE

What qualifies anyone for God's grace? Nothing—only grace itself. Do you trust God and rest yourself on Christ alone? Is he, plus nothing, your hope? Then come to this Table and receive the bread and wine, signs of his sacrifice offered for you. You belong to him by the name he placed on you in baptism. You live in the fellowship of his church and its wholesome accountability. But deeper than these things is your felt need of his presence. God himself has opened heaven to you by the blood of Jesus (see Heb. 10:19). Come, enter the holy place, eat and drink with the Lord Jesus Christ. The apostle Paul wrote, "For I received from the Lord what I also delivered to you, that the Lord Jesus on the night when he was betrayed took bread . . ." (1 Cor. 11:23–26).

Of course, these are only meant to be suggestive. Maintaining these elements in inviting, every pastor will develop words that express his own faith in Christ's blessing on the sacrament along with his guidance for his people.

WARNING

When Paul corrected the Corinthian church so they might stop abusing the Lord's Supper, he required that each one "examine" himself (1 Cor. 11:28). What was the object of that examination? Each one was to see that he understood the meaning of the body and the blood of Christ given for us. Do we trust Christ alone for salvation and live in love for our neighbors? The purpose of this examination is not that we should *abstain* from the Table. The purpose is that we should *come* to it with confidence in Christ ("and so eat"; 1 Cor. 11:28). In other words, we are to come with joy, because we find ourselves trusting Christ the Savior and reconciled to others.[7]

---

7 In the context of sixteenth-century scholastic theology, John Calvin warned against an introspection that *prevented* believers from eating: "Commonly, when they would prepare men to eat worthily, they have tortured and harassed pitiable consciences in dire ways. . . . They said that those that were in state of grace ate worthily. They interpreted 'in state of grace' to mean to be pure and purged from all sin. Such a dogma would debar all the men who ever were or are on earth from use of this sacrament. For if it is a question of our seeking worthiness by ourselves, we are undone; only despair and deadly ruin remain to us. Although we try with all our strength, we shall make no headway, except that in the end we shall be most unworthy, after we have labored mightily in pursuit of worthiness" (*Inst.*, 2:1418 [4/17.41]).

Eating and drinking assume a certain ability of spiritual judgment: Scripture requires us to discern the body (1 Cor. 11:29), meaning the spiritual significance of the bread and the cup of the Lord (v. 27). Is this just another bit of food, or is it an actual fellowship with Christ in this sacrificial meal? It is the latter. Thus the Supper is a most solemn event. We are to come with deep joy and with deep solemnity. When I write "solemnity," I mean importance, significance, and gravity. Think, for example, of a wedding. For most of us, there is no happier event. The celebration and joy are appropriate to the solemnity of the vows that bride and groom have made to God. The vows are permanent. God is their witness and help to lifelong devotion. We celebrate with joy.[8] We are to come to this Table with profound joy.

The same servant's attitude that led Christ obediently to death "should pervade the Supper for Christians ever after."[9] The meal is a sharing in the new covenant, which binds God's people into one. Paul warned the church not to eat in an "unworthy manner" (v. 27). This had no reference to moral deserving or righteousness.[10] Instead the question was one of "inappropriate" eating. This is not a normal meal at which one may casually, or worse, arrogantly, eat and drink, because God will judge the person who treats the body and blood of Christ as something common.[11]

It is important to maintain balance in interpreting verse 29. Some understand Paul's warning, "anyone who eats and drinks without discerning the body," as referring solely to the way we are to treat each

---

8 Good custom has it that we are to look each other in the eyes as we drink a toast!

9 David E. Garland, *1 Corinthians*, Baker Exegetical Commentary on the New Testament, ed. Robert W. Yarbrough and Robert H. Stein (Grand Rapids: Baker Book House, 2003), 550.

10 Herman N. Ridderbos, *Paul: An Outline of His Theology*, trans. John R. deWitt (Grand Rapids: Eerdmans, 1975), 425.

11 Ridderbos writes, "Whoever does not respect the sanctity of this table fellowship, therefore, will be guilty of Christ's body and blood, that is to say, sin against the sacrifice made by him. . . . He who at the table does not respect the sacrifice of the Crucified falls under the judgment of the exalted Lord" (ibid., 426).

other in the church, the "body" of Christ.[12] This is certainly a vital matter. Their ill treatment of each other at the Supper had prompted Paul to rebuke the church at Corinth. God was actually bringing judgment to "many" in the Corinthian church (v. 30). Verses 21–22 indicate that there was a humiliating of the poor brethren of the church and so a shaming of them ("one goes hungry"), as well as overindulgence in the meal ("another gets drunk").[13] The behavior of the wealthy was divisive and thus it undermined the very meaning of the Lord's Supper. In the previous chapter, Paul had affirmed that "because there is one bread, we who are many are one body, for we all partake of the one bread" (1 Cor. 10:17). These words are the background of chapter 11. The church would normally have broken one loaf of bread and shared it as one group, not as "separated" individuals or an "in-group." Some in Corinth "had found a way of participating in the Lord's Supper that completely undermined that part of its message."[14] God responded in judgment.

Still, it is more likely that Paul's phrase "discerning the body" in 11:29 refers to the meaning of the Supper itself, because he writes in verse 27 that the one who eats unworthily "will be guilty concerning the body *and blood* of the Lord" not just "the body" (meaning the church). Christ's sacrifice of body and blood for us all makes us one body. So we should see in Paul's warning that the sacrificial significance of the meal, along with the community that the sacrifice has created, is in view. The two must not be pulled apart.

---

12 See Wayne Grudem, *Systematic Theology: An Introduction to Biblical Doctrine* (Grand Rapids: Zondervan, 1994), 997.

13 In Corinth, "the bread of the Lord" most likely opened the Supper, and the "cup of the Lord" closed it. At the meal in between, the wealthier members of the community, by not sharing, cared only for themselves and thus undermined the entire meaning of the Lord's Supper. See Otfried Hofius, "The Lord's Supper and the Lord's Supper Tradition: Reflections on 1 Corinthians 11:23b–25," in *One Loaf, One Cup: Ecumenical Studies of 1 Cor 11 and Other Eucharistic Texts*, ed. Ben F. Meyer (Macon, GA: Mercer University Press, 1993), 96.

14 Roy E. Ciampa and Brian S. Rosner, *The First Letter to the Corinthians*, The Pillar New Testament Commentary, ed. D. A. Carson (Grand Rapids: Eerdmans, 2010), 552.

Likewise, we should note that the judgment in Corinth was a "chastening," not a condemnation. There is no more condemnation for those who are in Christ Jesus (Rom. 8:1). Chastening is a wholesome discipline (no less painful for that) intended to lead God's church to deepened faith and repentance (see Heb. 12:5–6). It produces good, righteous fruit. But in any event, Paul urges believers to test themselves so that they might not be chastened. That chastening is of utmost seriousness.[15] As Thomas Boston once confessed, "His frowns are as bitter as death."[16]

---

15 The question of the admission of baptized children to the Lord's Table before they profess faith in Christ, called "paedocommunion," is controversial in Presbyterian and Reformed churches. A case is made that small children ate the Passover meal in Israel, that they are members of God's covenant people, and that therefore they have a right to the Lord's Table. The issue is more complex than what I can discuss here. But Paul's statement that those who partake "proclaim the Lord's death until he comes" (1 Cor. 11:26) requires that they be able to understand and to "announce" the importance of Jesus' death, as well as expect his return. Likewise, the requirement that persons "examine" themselves and so eat (v. 28) seems to limit the invitation to those who are able publicly to profess faith in Christ. That is the position of the Westminster Larger Catechism, question and answer 177. However, the age at which children are able to profess faith may be quite young. For an excellent treatment of this question, see Vern S. Poythress, "Indifferentism and Rigorism in the Church: With Implications for Baptizing Small Children," *Westminster Theological Journal* 59, no. 1 (1997): 13–29. And for a magisterial treatment of the biblical and theological issues regarding "paedocommunion," see Cornelis P. Venema, *Children at the Lord's Table? Assessing the Case for Paedocommunion* (Grand Rapids: Reformation Heritage, 2009).

16 Thomas Boston, *Memoirs of Thomas Boston* (1899; repr., Edinburgh: Banner of Truth, 1988), 117.

CHAPTER THREE

Basic Themes

The Lord's Supper has a basic structure, a meaning given to it by God in the New Testament. Paul lays out this structure in 1 Corinthians 11:23–26. He introduces it in his letter to correct the church's abuses (11:22). This should not distract us from the fact that the character of the words indicates that they are "words of institution" (he introduces them with the conjunction "for"), and thus to be followed in all that we say at the Table.

Paul traces the traditional form of words back to Jesus himself. He received it from the exalted Christ ("from the Lord" and "the Lord Jesus," v. 23)[1] and passed it on as apostolic tradition to be followed.[2] The apostles served as authoritative representatives of Christ, and Paul's point in verse 23 is that the Supper tradition is to be followed by the church (as the Corinthians should *already* have been doing). Several things characterize the administration of the Supper.

The Lord Jesus was the host, the giver, and the one who administered the meal. This he still does. The Lord hands the bread and

---

1 He does not specify the means of this reception, though it was certainly through the words of the Last Supper later recorded in the Gospels. For major studies of the relationship between these words and the gospel accounts, see Joachim Jeremias, *The Eucharistic Words of Jesus*, trans. Norman Perrin (1977; repr., Philadelphia: Fortress, 1981); and I. Howard Marshall, *Last Supper and Lord's Supper* (London: Paternoster, 1980; repr. Vancouver, Canada: Regent College, 2006).

2 See 1 Corinthians 15:3 for the same description of "passing on" his gospel. As apostle, Paul spoke with the authority of Christ to the church. For a brief but stimulating discussion of the character of the New Testament apostle, see Richard B. Gaffin Jr., *Perspectives on Pentecost: New Testament Teaching on the Gifts of the Holy Spirit* (Phillipsburg, NJ: Presbyterian and Reformed, 1979), 89–93.

the cup to his disciples as the host of the meal.[3] Jesus gave thanks to God (εὐχαριστήσας, *eucharistēsas*, v. 24)[4] at the last Passover, as the father of a family would have done. He did this before he broke the bread and distributed it to the disciples. The prayer would have been thanksgiving for God's provision and for God's great salvation accomplished in the exodus from Egypt.[5] However, in 1 Corinthians 10:16, Paul refers to the "bread that *we* break," and the cup that "*we* bless"; that is, as Christians. This implies that Paul gave thanks not for the exodus of Israel but, as a Christian, for the redemption accomplished by Jesus' death.[6] (The two are related, of course, as the type and its eschatological fulfillment.) The Westminster Confession of Faith calls the Supper "a spiritual oblation of all possible praise" (29.2) for Jesus' self-offering. Ministers should follow Jesus' practice with deep laudation and thanks in their prayers.

A shadow fell over Jesus' last Passover: it took place "on the night when he was betrayed" (1 Cor. 11:23). "Delivered up" is also a possible rendering, though it is less likely, since Jesus announced his betrayal at the Last Supper. Still, it is worth noting that Paul uses the same verb in Romans 4:25 and 8:32 (see also the Greek translation of Isa. 53:12), referring to the Father's "giving up" of his Son to death. Surely the Father's plan lay behind Judas' betrayal (see Acts 2:23–24). In verse 23 Paul calls the Corinthian church to recognize and join the great solemnity of this meal. Jesus' sufferings were in his view as he graciously set this Table for his own.

---

3 This is in contrast to his *having received* the previous Passover cup (Luke 22:17).

4 So Paul and Mark 14:23 and Luke 22:19–20, while Matthew (26:26) writes "blessing" in connection with the cup. The verbs should be understood as equivalent.

5 Ciampa and Rosner comment, "In the shadow of that death, Christ still recognized God's faithful and generous provision for him and his disciples as he shared his last meal with them" (Roy E. Ciampa and Brian S. Rosner, *The First Letter to the Corinthians*, The Pillar New Testament Commentary, ed. D. A. Carson [Grand Rapids: Eerdmans, 2010], 550).

6 See Leonhard Goppelt, *Theology of the New Testament*, vol. 2, *The Variety and Unity of the Apostolic Witness to Christ*, trans. John Alsup, ed. Jurgen Roloff (Grand Rapids: Eerdmans, 1982), 148. Differing with Goppelt, I do not take the prayer as a "consecration."

Jesus then spoke of the bread (v. 24): "This is my body which is for you."[7] "Body" in this phrase refers to the body of Jesus given over to death on the cross. The prepositional phrase "for you" (τὸ ὑπὲρ ὑμῶν, *to hyper hymōn*) describes specifically Jesus' self-surrender to death, as a substitute, for the expiation of sin. This is Paul's constant use of the phrase (cf. especially 15:3 "for our sins").[8] It is important to note again that the "bread saying" and the "cup saying" must be understood *together* as referring to Jesus' propitiatory death.[9] In other words, the nourishing quality of the bread is found only as the result of Jesus' death, which removed God's righteous wrath against sin. Eating the bread (with the wine) is sharing the effect of Jesus' death: the forgiveness of sins.[10] The "you" is plural. Jesus gave his body for the whole church. No believer may be excluded or humiliated.

Jesus' words, "Do this" (v. 24b), are a command to repeat the thanksgiving, breaking, and distribution of the bread and wine and the words of explanation. What is the thrust of Jesus' words "in remembrance of me" (repeated in v. 25)?

God established the Passover as a "memorial" feast (Ex. 12:14), during which Israel was to remember the great acts of God redeeming them from Egypt. "Seven days you shall eat it with unleavened bread, the bread of affliction—for you came out of the land of Egypt in

---

7 The words "for you" are an adaptation of Isaiah 53:12 in the Septuagint. Cf. Luke 22:19—"given for you."

8 Romans 5:6, 8; 8:32; 14:15; 1 Corinthians 1:13; 2 Corinthians 5:14–15; Galatians 2:20; 1 Thessalonians 5:10; cited by Otfried Hofius, "The Lord's Supper and the Lord's Supper Tradition: Reflections on 1 Corinthians 11:23b–25," in *One Loaf, One Cup: Ecumenical Studies of 1 Cor 11 and Other Eucharistic Texts*, ed. Ben F. Meyer (Macon, GA: Mercer University Press, 1993), 98n129.

9 "Cf. the juxtaposition and conjunction of the two notions of Christ's 'body' and 'blood' in Col. 1:20, 22 as well as the epistle to the Hebrews (σῶμα, *sōma*, 10:5, 10; αἷμα, *haima*, 9:12, 14; 10:19, 29; 12:24; 13:12)" (ibid., 99n131).

10 Despite his unfortunate reservations about Pauline authorship of some of the thirteen canonical letters, Hofius helpfully notes that references to Jesus' blood in the New Testament "regularly express the expiatory efficacy of his death: see Acts 20:28; Eph. 1:7; 2:13; Col. 1:20; Heb. 9:12, 14; 10:19, 29; 12:24; 13:12; 1 Peter 1:2, 19; 1 John 1:7; 5:6, 8; Rev. 1:5; 5:9; 7:14; 12:11" (ibid., 99n130).

haste—that all the days of your life you may remember the day when you came out of the land of Egypt" (Deut. 16:3). The father would explain to his family that the Lord had redeemed them in the exodus. God's mighty redemption was to be in the consciousness of every following generation. "When your children say to you, 'What do you mean by this service?' you shall say, 'It is the sacrifice of the LORD's Passover, for he passed over the houses of the people of Israel in Egypt, when he struck the Egyptians but spared our houses'" (Ex. 12:26–27).[11] There was to be thoughtful recognition of the great saving act of God and its present meaning. They were God's saved people.

In the Psalms, to "remember" God's great deeds (Ps. 77:11–12) was to remember God himself, and even to proclaim his name. It involved the whole life of covenant obedience and praise to the Lord. Hofius notes that remembering is found side by side with proclaiming in Psalm 105, "*Remember the wondrous works* that he has done, his miracles, and the judgments he uttered" (v. 5) and "Oh give thanks to the LORD; call upon his name; *make known his deeds* among the peoples!" (v. 1), which he calls "praise-filled proclamation."[12] If we notice the rich content of the psalmists' remembering (God's "acts," "faithfulness," "goodness," "righteousness"; see Ps. 9:1; 89:1; 145:4–7; and so on), we are prompted to think, with them, of the many aspects of what the Lord Jesus has done for us in his death and resurrection. This is the background of Jesus' command, "Remember me." Ridderbos summarizes: "Christ's self-surrender is now, as hitherto the exodus of Israel out of Egypt, the new and definitive fact of redemption, which in the eating of the bread and in the drinking of the wine, the church may accept as such again and again from the hand of God."[13]

---

11 Cf. the words of Deuteronomy 6:21: "We were Pharaoh's slaves in Egypt. And the LORD brought us out of Egypt with a mighty hand." Ciampa and Rosner quote the Passover seder, in which the father explained to his son, "'because of that which the Lord did for me when I came forth out of Egypt,' (*m. Peshahim* 10:5)" (*First Letter to the Corinthians*, 551).

12 Hofius, "Lord's Supper," 106.

13 Ridderbos, *Paul*, 421.

Jesus commanded us to remember in the eating and the drinking. Paul, as he draws an inference from this in 1 Corinthians 11:26 ("for"), calls this "proclamation": "As often as you eat this bread and drink the cup, you proclaim the Lord's death until he comes." Clearly, then, it is the resurrected Christ of whom Paul speaks ("the Lord," and the reference to his coming). Eating and drinking is acknowledging and embracing the significance of Jesus' saving death and his manifold and continued grace to us.

He is present with us as the Lord of the new covenant. When we drink, we share that covenant with him. That is the content of verse 25, "This cup is the new covenant in my blood." The wine in the cup stands for Jesus' shed blood. Jesus' statement "fuses together"[14] the language of Jeremiah 31:31, "Behold, the days are coming, declares the LORD, when I will make a new covenant with the house of Israel and the house of Judah," and Exodus 24:8, "Behold the blood of the covenant that the LORD has made with you." The latter text refers to the blood of sacrifice sprinkled on the people to ratify the covenant at Sinai. But Jeremiah had predicted a *new* covenant that would bring about "perfect communion with God in his reign (Jer. 31:33–34a), based on the remission of sins (Jer. 31:34b)."[15] Jesus was saying that his blood shedding would cause this new covenant to go into effect.

The sprinkled blood of Exodus 24:3–8 signified that God and Israel were mutually bound to each other. God had sovereignly redeemed them, and he called them to live as his sons (Ex. 4:22–23). The sprinkled blood of sacrifice indicated God's cleansing along with the people's consecration to serve God on pain of death. The blood shed by Jesus fulfills the symbolism of that sacrificial blood with actual redemption in history. As O. Palmer Robertson writes, "Not only does Christ's blood remove the curse of the old covenant;

---

14 Ciampa and Rosner, *First Letter to the Corinthians*, 552.
15 Jeremias, *Eucharistic Words*, 226. Matthew 26:28 gives the fuller statement: "for the forgiveness of sins."

simultaneously it introduces the blessed condition of the new covenant."[16] Again, Jesus' interpretation of the cup is that his shed blood enacted the final salvation promised by Jeremiah: forgiveness of sins and fellowship with God.[17] We may certainly say that whatever is included in the new covenant is included in the representation of the cup of Jesus' blood. At the cross, Jesus set the new and final age in motion. We are the partakers of that wonderful salvation. In 1 Corinthians 10:16, Paul writes, "The cup of blessing that we bless, is it not a participation in the blood of Christ?" When we eat and drink, we have fellowship with Christ himself, and we have the benefits of his death. God has made these provisions for his people in the new covenant.

Those who drink the cup of the Lord in the church should be those who recognize the character of his blood shed on the cross. We must also be those who keep, by faith and by the Spirit, the new covenant. Since Christ has redeemed all God's people, we are to accept everyone and show no favoritism. This too is proclaimed in the Supper.

The Supper is the meal of the new covenant in which we joyfully acknowledge the redemption accomplished by Christ's death and receive the signs of our participation in him. We do that as we await his return "until he comes." We live in the period between his great redeeming cross and our glorified eating and drinking in the kingdom of God (Matt. 26:29; Mark 14:25; Luke 22:16).

The great meal of all God's redeemed people in the kingdom of God, the wedding supper of the Lamb, is coming. Jesus' death guaranteed that. So as we look back with faith, we look ahead also with faith to that great day.

In sum, then, each observance of the Lord's Supper must stress

---

16 O. Palmer Robertson, *The Christ of the Covenants* (Phillipsburg, NJ: Presbyterian and Reformed, 1980), 145.

17 Jeremias, *Eucharistic Words*, 169. That Jesus' death actually accomplished all the benefits of the new covenant is pervasively taught in the book of Hebrews: 9:11–12, 24–26, 28; 10:10, 12, 14, 18; 13:12.

(1) that the exalted Lord is the minister at his Table. There he distributes the bread and wine, (2) by which, through faith, we participate in the benefits of his substitutionary death. With great and solemn joy, we remember him, proclaim his redemption to all, and offer him all possible praise. (3) For on the cross he redeemed for God a people to whom he is bound by the new and final covenant. (4) As inaugurating that covenant, his sacrifice was for the whole church. (5) Our sins are forgiven in his blood, and our future is secured in his blood. (6) He will come for us to welcome us to the great feast of glory. Along with the church in the New Testament, we are those who have "turned to God from idols to serve the living and true God, and to wait for his Son from heaven, whom he raised from the dead, Jesus who delivers us from the wrath to come" (1 Thess. 1:9–10).

PART TWO

Meditations at the Lord's Table

CHAPTER FOUR

Old Covenant Anticipations

PASSOVER PROVISION
─ *Exodus 12:27* ─

Before God brought his people out of Egypt, he instituted a yearly feast, the Passover. Its purpose was to remind Israel of his grace in redeeming them in their history. We read about the first Passover in Exodus chapter 12.

God protected Israel from all the judgment plagues on Egypt. The plagues did not fall on them. In the climactic tenth plague, the rod of judgment was raised against the Egyptians, whose firstborn were threatened with death. But if God's judgment required the death of the sinner, how could Israel survive that threat? Surely they were sinners too. Despite God's distinguishing grace, their final redemption from bondage could be accomplished only by an atoning sacrifice.

Back in Genesis, when God had required the death of Isaac, Abraham's firstborn, God himself provided a substitute (Gen. 22:8). Abraham sacrificed the ram instead of his beloved son (Gen. 22:13).

Through Moses, God commanded that each household choose a lamb from the flock. It had to be spotless, perfect (Ex. 12:5). "It is the sacrifice of the LORD's Passover, for he passed over the houses of the people of Israel in Egypt, when he struck the Egyptians but spared our houses" (Ex. 12:27). The lambs were slaughtered and the blood sprinkled with hyssop on the doorposts. On the night that the angel of death passed over, the firstborn in those homes were spared. The smearing of the blood on the doorposts with hyssop signaled purification from the stain of guilt. God saw the blood and his justice was satisfied.[1]

Why do we need a sacrifice? We need it because of sin. Not because of just "a sin" here or there, but because in the deepest recesses of our hearts we have constantly rebelled against and offended our God. That was the bent of our life. And yet, because of his great love for us, he provided a perfect, sinless sacrifice, that the bondage of our hearts might be removed and that we might receive his blessing again.

Now, in the age of God's kingdom, it is not the Israelite families, nor we, who provide a lamb; it is God himself who has provided the Lamb.

Jesus Christ was the true Lamb provided by God. His spotlessness was much more than the physical purity of a lamb. It was his life of perfect obedience. "My food is to do the will of him who sent me and to accomplish his work" (John 4:34). Peter tells us, "He committed no sin, neither was deceit found in his mouth" (1 Peter 2:22). He writes, "You were ransomed from the futile ways inherited from your forefathers, not with perishable things such as silver or gold, but with the precious blood of Christ, like that of a lamb without blemish or spot" (1 Peter 1:18–19).

From eternity, the Father had infinite delight in his precious Son. Peter wrote that Jesus had now fulfilled all his will. Thus his blood was precious to God, as only his own Son's blood could be. The sacrifice perfectly satisfied all God's requirements for us.

---

1 "The blood sprinkled on the doorposts and lintels of the Israelites was not there to impress the Egyptians. It was there to attract the attention of God so that the angel of judgment would pass the marked households by (Exod. 12:13)" (Donald Macleod, *Christ Crucified: Understanding the Atonement* [Downers Grove, IL: InterVarsity Press, 2014], 72).

For Israel, the Passover lamb was a sacrifice for sin and a peace offering.[2] Their feast of blessing and joy rested on the sacrifice that the Lord made for them. God was reconciled.

Year by year, God reminded the people with the Passover feast. The meal included bitter herbs to renew the bitter memory of living under the domination of foreign gods. The Passover testified that they owed their existence as a people, and all their blessings in Canaan, to the grace of blood-bought redemption. They enjoyed union with the Trinity and salvation by Christ, even before his incarnation in history. We, of course, have so much more—the fullness of Christ's ministry as crucified and risen, and our union with him.

These are the signs of the blood-bought redemption that the Passover lamb promised. "He himself bore our sins in his body on the tree. . . . By his wounds you have been healed" (1 Peter 2:24). Receive the signs of Christ's atonement, eat his body, and drink his blood with joy today. Your God has redeemed you. He is reconciled. You have forgiveness from the past and freedom for the new life in Christ. Enjoy, by faith, his gracious fellowship.

CHRIST OUR PASSOVER
— *1 Corinthians 5:7–8* —

The feasts of the Old Testament confirmed God's great salvation for believing Israelites. The Passover, especially, reminded them of God's power and grace in the exodus. The sacrifice of a lamb or a goat from the flock, with its blood sprinkled on the door with hyssop, was a sign of salvation by a substitute. The feast itself was joyful fellowship with the God of the covenant, who had saved them from judgment. They were to tell each generation of the family: "It is the sacrifice of

---

2 See Geerhardus Vos, *Biblical Theology: Old and New Testaments* (Grand Rapids: Eerdmans, 1948; Edinburgh: Banner of Truth, 1975), 120. Citations refer to the reprint edition.

the LORD's Passover, for he passed over the houses of the people of Israel in Egypt, when he struck the Egyptians but spared our houses" (Ex. 12:27).

Their feasting expressed the joy of peace with God. Blessing and joy rested on the sacrifice the Lord made for them. God was reconciled. The Feast of Unleavened Bread was also part of the first Passover meal. The bread had to be unleavened because they were about to leave the old life and begin the new. God even changed their calendar—from now on this was the beginning of the year (Ex. 12:1)! Their new life in Canaan was a holy life with God.

In Corinth, we learn, the church was foolishly boasting about an instance of immorality. Paul wrote that it should have made them weep. Their freedom in Christ was not freedom to live in sin. Paul reminds them of the fulfillment of the Passover sacrifice. The curse that fell on the firstborn of Egypt was fulfilled in the final curse that fell on Jesus Christ.

> Cleanse out the old leaven that you may be a new lump, as you really are unleavened. For Christ, our Passover lamb, has been sacrificed. Let us therefore celebrate the festival, not with the old leaven, the leaven of malice and evil, but with the unleavened bread of sincerity and truth. (1 Cor. 5:7–8)

The suffering and death of the Son of God as our substitute, his body and blood given for us, is the means by which we have received forgiveness of sins, peace of conscience, and fellowship with God. And, likewise, Christ's new resurrection life belongs to us in him. Like the Corinthians, we are a "new lump," and so we are to "become unleavened, by repenting of sin and walking in a holy life. We can never earn God's favor, but neither can we ignore the sin that offends God. "Become what you are in Christ," is Paul's constant command.

When we receive Christ by faith, we are joined to him. His death belongs to us by faith. So also does his resurrection life. The two cannot be separated. Peter puts it like this: "He himself bore our sins in his body on the tree, that we might die to sin and live to righteousness" (1 Peter 2:24).

Take and eat this bread, as God's sign to you that Christ died for you and that he nourishes you today by his Spirit. Trust in the forgiveness of all your sins, and rejoice. Drink the cup as God seals to your heart the fellowship that you have with Christ. The old things have passed away. Look—the new things have come! Our whole life is a feasting with the Lord. Take, eat, remember, and believe that the body of our Lord Jesus Christ was given for you.

This Is the Blood of the Covenant
— *Exodus 24:8* —

At the Last Supper, Jesus called his own blood the "blood of the covenant": "This is my blood of the covenant, which is poured out for many" (Matt. 26:28). With these words, he referred to God's covenant making on Mount Sinai in Exodus 24.

The covenant at Sinai formalized the relationship of promise that God made with Abraham and his children (Gen. 12, 15, 17, 18, 22). God had redeemed his people from Egypt, as he promised Abraham (Gen. 15:14). The exodus showed his power and grace to the twelve tribes of Abraham's family. He spoke of his saving acts at the beginning of the Ten Commandments: "I am the Lord your God, who brought you out of the land of Egypt, out of the house of slavery" (Ex. 20:2). The commandments that followed were God's instruction for his redeemed people. Now, at Sinai, God renewed the committed relationship of grace. Moses the mediator set up twelve pillars, representing the twelve tribes (Ex. 24:4).

The event included the reading of the law.[3] God instructed his people in his will for their life in the land, their life in fellowship with him. He expressed his sovereign authority in these rules. These were the terms of the covenant relationship: God's redemption, his dwelling in their midst in the tabernacle, and the life of God's people, walking in obedience to him. Because the covenant includes their response, the assent of the people was required. The whole people responded to the reading, "All that the LORD has spoken we will do, and we will be obedient" (24:7; see also 19:5, 8). God wants us to respond to his will in willing obedience.

The ratification ceremony followed, made up of the same two elements that we found in the Passover: the sacrifice and the fellowship meal.

Moses set up an altar and the twelve pillars. He had young men sacrifice burnt offerings and peace offerings. Then he took the blood of sacrifice, put half of it in basins, and threw the other half against the altar. This represented expiation of the sins of the people. Having made this offering for the people, "Moses took the blood and threw it on the people and said, 'Behold the blood of the covenant that the LORD has made with you in accordance with all these words'" (24:8). The sprinkled blood symbolized the purification of the people, and it consecrated them to keep the covenant on the pain of death.

Then Scripture tells us that there was an amazing meal.

Moses and Aaron, Nadab, and Abihu, and seventy of the elders of Israel went up, and they saw the God of Israel. There was under his feet as it were a pavement of sapphire stone, like the very heaven for clearness. And he did not lay his hand on the chief men of the people of Israel; they beheld God, and ate and drank. (vv. 9–11)

---

3 Throughout Scripture, the ceremonies of covenant renewal repeat this practice. See Joshua 24, 2 Kings 23, and Nehemiah 8.

Through the covenant making, the Lord had become "the God of Israel" in a new way. Normally it was dangerous, even fatal, for people to see God. But in this case the relationship, forged in sacrificial blood, was so close that "he did not lay his hand" on them.[4] Later the prophets of Israel saw a greater meal on the mountain of God, which would include all the nations (Isa. 25:6–8). The writer to the Hebrews considered this cleansing at Sinai just an anticipation of the final cleansing that Jesus' blood has now brought, because he brings us into heaven itself (Heb. 9:18–26).

The bread and wine that Jesus set apart express the fulfilled covenant relationship, because the shed blood is not the blood of animals but his own blood. Today God will seal on your heart his bond with you, the perfect fellowship brought about by Jesus' blood, "my blood of the covenant." God will never lift up his hand against you, because he lifted it against Jesus. Because God raised Jesus on the third day, one day he will raise your body. Entrust yourself again to the final, perfect Mediator, Jesus Christ. Rejoice in his faithfulness and offer yourself to him as a living sacrifice.

The Great Feast
— *Isaiah 25:6–8* —

When God brought Israel through the sea and entered into covenant with them at Sinai, the elders ate and drank with him. "They saw the God of Israel" (apparently only partially—cf. the pavement under his feet, Ex. 24:10–11). The elders represented Israel as the covenant was consummated with their Savior. Sadly, by their constant disobedience, the nation broke the covenant and lost their privilege through exile. But God did not change his purpose. Isaiah promised that on Mount Zion God would make a feast for all nations.

---

4 Possibly some limit is expressed, because they saw only God's "feet" (v. 10).

At this banquet, all the restrictions will be lifted. Not just the elders but also all the people will be there. Not just the people but also the Gentile nations will be there. The whole earth will be there as "his people" (Isa. 25:8). Isaiah uses the words "peoples" (v. 6), or ethnic groups, "nations" (v. 7), or political entities, and "faces" (v. 8), or individuals.[5] God will provide banqueting fare of unimaginable richness. There will be gourmet food and the finest wine, well aged. What a meal!

But the finest food is not much good if you have to eat alone. We rarely have the opportunity to feast with all the people who we love most. For whatever reasons, we are scattered. Worst of all, death separates us from those we love. But, Isaiah wrote, on that day God will remove the "shroud" that covers all peoples. "He will swallow up death forever; and . . . wipe away tears from all faces" (v. 8). God will rescue us from our most relentless enemy. The reproach of death's curse will be gone; there will be nothing but life, nothing but resurrection joy in God's presence. We will be reunited with the whole body of Christ. No regrets, no sorrow on that day. The amazing beauty of that fellowship meal is beyond our grasp. But Isaiah tells us of the song: "Behold, this is our God; we have waited for him, that he might save us. This is the LORD; we have waited for him; let us be glad and rejoice in his salvation" (v. 9). We will give God the praise he is due. He will comfort us. Our joy and the Father's will be one.

Banquets are not so fine if those who we love are suffering. A Roman soldier had asked Jesus to heal his paralyzed servant. The centurion refused Jesus' offer to come and heal him, replying, "I am not worthy to have you come under my roof, but only say the word, and my servant will be healed" (Matt. 8:8). Jesus answered with wonder. No Israelite had faith like this Gentile. Did the centurion ask the Messiah's help because he understood that Jesus was about removing the curse from the creation? Was he looking forward to the banquet

---

5 J. Alec Motyer, *The Prophecy of Isaiah: An Introduction and Commentary* (Downers Grove, IL: InterVarsity Press, 1993), 209.

on the mountain? We do not know. But in joy Jesus said, "I tell you, many will come from east and west and recline at table with Abraham, Isaac, and Jacob in the kingdom of heaven, while the sons of the kingdom will be thrown into the outer darkness" (Matt. 8:11–12). Then he healed the centurion's servant with a word. Jesus was gathering sinners from Israel and from the Gentiles; they were destined for the great banquet. Pagan kings had already come from the east, and Rome lay to the west.[6]

Jesus continues to gather until the full number has come to faith. What a gathering! Father Abraham with all his children, in fulfillment of every covenant promise. Every believer from all ages, and every nation of earth, will be there in resurrected glory. Jesus will be there. And God will be all in all. We will see him face to face.

The Table at which we gather today is a foretaste of that banquet. Edmund P. Clowney wrote, "The Lord's Supper anticipates the messianic banquet because it marks the atoning blood of Christ through which the feast is made ready and its guests brought in."[7] Death separates God's family and casts its shadow over our lives. But Jesus Christ endured that death in our place. And God raised him, never to die again. So will he raise us. One day we will be reunited forever.

Eat and drink today in the sure confidence that soon you will eat and drink with all the beloved in your Father's kingdom.

My Servant Shall Be Exalted
— *Isaiah 52:13* —

At the Last Supper, Jesus said of the cup, "This is my blood of the covenant, which is poured out for many for the forgiveness of sins"

---

6 Craig L. Blomberg, *Contagious Holiness: Jesus' Meals with Sinners*, New Studies in Biblical Theology 19, ed. D. A. Carson (Downers Grove, IL: InterVarsity Press, 2005), 113.

7 Edmund P. Clowney, *The Church*, Contours of Biblical Theology, ed. Gerald Bray (Downers Grove, IL: InterVarsity Press, 1994), 285.

(Matt. 26:28). By using the words "the blood of the covenant" (words that repeat Ex. 24:8), Jesus alluded to the Sinai covenant. But notice also that he added the word "my": "my blood of the covenant, which is poured out for many." He was referring to the prophecy of the Servant of the Lord in Isaiah 53. Jesus would fulfill God's word of prophecy about the Servant in Isaiah 52:13–53:12.[8] (We are familiar with Isaiah 53, because the evangelists and apostles quote it as many as seven times.) God's covenant included the plan to save his people by the sufferings of the Servant. The song consists of an introduction (52:13–15) and four stanzas. These predict, in alternating order, the events of Jesus' sufferings, followed by their interpretation, their rationale, in God's plan.[9]

What we may not have noticed is that Isaiah begins and ends the prophecy by writing not about the Servant's sufferings but about his exaltation after death (52:13–15; 53:10–12). Jesus was no mere tragic figure; instead, God intended to raise him from the dead and install him as mighty saving Lord of the universe. There was a deep rationale for Jesus' sufferings. The Lord speaks personally about him: "Behold, my servant shall act wisely[10]; he shall be high and lifted up, and shall be exalted" (52:13); "the will of the LORD shall prosper in his hand" (53:10).

His sufferings would be very severe: "As many were astonished at you—his appearance was so marred, beyond human semblance, and his form beyond that of the children of mankind . . . as one from whom men hide their faces he was despised" (52:14; 53:3). But those sufferings were precious to God. God would not leave it there. God would reward him. In fact, he would cleanse many of the rulers of the earth, and they would serve him in obedience: "so shall he sprinkle

---

8 The fourth so-called "Servant Song" in Isaiah, along with 42:1–9; 49:1–13; 50:4–9.

9 See Henri Blocher, *Songs of the Servant: Isaiah's Good News* (London: Inter-Varsity Press, 1975), 61.

10 Or "shall prosper" (see note on Isaiah 52:13 in ESV).

many nations; kings shall shut their mouths because of him" (52:15)
Further in the song, Isaiah 53:10 helps us to understand the word
"sprinkle." "When his soul makes an offering for guilt" refers to the
Mosaic sin offering, the blood of which the priest was to sprinkle
before the altar (Lev. 4:6). Through this offering, many sinners would
find cleansing. In the New Testament, Peter wrote to believers in Asia
Minor, chosen, "according to the foreknowledge of God the Father, in
the sanctification of the Spirit, for obedience to Jesus Christ and for
sprinkling with his blood" (1 Peter 1:2). God did it. As believers, you
have received that sprinkling of his blood.

Again, at the end of the song, God speaks of his plan to glorify
the Servant. "Therefore I will divide him a portion with the many,
and he shall divide the spoil with the strong, because he poured out
his soul to death and was numbered with the transgressors" (53:12).
Jesus Christ would receive great rewards for his sufferings.

It was he, the one who would be glorified, who established this
meal on the night he was betrayed. So we eat with joy, not with sorrow. Our hearts are deeply moved to thank God for this plan. He
gave his Son for our sins. Christ "poured out his soul to death." He
willingly put himself in our place as the Servant of the Lord's will.

How thankful we should be, as we eat and drink today, that God
designed this plan; that Jesus did, in fact, suffer for us; and that God
raised him and exalted him to the place of glory at his right hand.
We celebrate his sufferings and his death. We acknowledge willingly
that we could not have accomplished peace with God from our side,
because we were all straying away from God and had no ability to
see Jesus' sufferings for what they were. But while we were blind and
dull, Jesus endured the hostility and evil of his enemies, because he
knew the Scriptures and knew that the will of his Father was to save
a needy people.

This underlines a very important part of the gospel. God was
acting to save us long before we believed or could do anything to

please him. His mere grace, fixed upon particular people, moved him to make this plan, to reveal it in Isaiah, and then to fulfill it in the life of his Son. It is not we who did something decisive, but God. Jesus Christ is the glorious Savior, and he has saved us. When Scripture says, "By grace you have been saved through faith" (Eph. 2:8), it means that we simply entrust ourselves to God as Savior.

Receive the bread and wine of the sacrifice made by the glorious King. Receive it from the King's hand. The will of the Lord is prospering in his hand as he saves you.

THE SUFFERINGS OF THE SERVANT
— Isaiah 53 —

This is not a very elaborate table—hardly a "feast." Almost all of us will probably enjoy a better menu today. But does this suggest that Christ is unworthy? In the second stanza of his song, Isaiah tells how unimpressive the Servant appeared—just a tiny shoot springing up from where the great cedars had been felled. He looked completely normal, not like a king or a savior (v. 2)—even though, in fact, in him God was revealing his "arm." (In Isa. 51:9, the "arm" of the Lord was God, saving his people in the exodus.) Instead the Servant would be utterly despised. His life was one marked by sorrow and grief. "He was despised and rejected by men; a man of sorrows, and acquainted with grief; and as one from whom men hide their faces he was despised, and we esteemed him not" (v. 3).

Personal acceptance, love, belonging—these are essential to joy. Yet people rejected the Servant. This was an accent of Jesus' experience. It was a real part of his sufferings. John's gospel tells us,

Though he had done so many signs before them, they still did not believe in him, so that the word spoken by the prophet Isaiah might be fulfilled:

"Lord, who has believed what he heard from us,
and to whom has the arm of the Lord been revealed?"
(John 12:37–38)

It is easy to dismiss someone who is suffering, and that was exactly the response to Jesus.

However, in verses 4–6 the Lord gives us the reasons for the Servant's sufferings, reasons which mere human appraisal could not grasp. What was the point? From a human point of view, there was no point. But he did not suffer for his own sins. Rather, he was a substitute. He did not "bear" or "carry" sorrows and infirmities for himself but did it for others (v. 4). In fact, these sufferings *were* completely unjust. Personally, he deserved nothing but reward. But his wounds and his being "crushed" were "for our transgressions" and "for our iniquities" (v. 5). Isaiah calls him "an offering for guilt" (v. 10). This is the same word used in Leviticus 5:16: "And the priest shall make atonement for him with the ram of the guilt offering, and he shall be forgiven."

Verses 4 and 12 tell us that the Servant suffered willingly and deliberately, not as the passive victim of injustice. He "took" our griefs. He "poured out his soul to death." He let himself be abused, accepting spitting, beating, bonds, and mockery from his captors (Isa. 50:6; Matt. 27:30; 26:67). In the process of his trial, he was led like a lamb to the slaughter, not opening his mouth in self-defense (Isa. 53:7; Matt. 27:12–14). He did not reply to or curse his enemies. In the New Testament, Peter echoes verse 9 in his description of Jesus: "He committed no sin, neither was deceit found in his mouth" (1 Peter 2:22).

But again we ask, why? It was God himself who acted to charge the people's sin to the Servant and to punish him. Verse 6 says, "The Lord has laid on him the iniquity of us all." It is more explicit still in verse 10: "It was the Lord's will to crush him and cause him to suffer" (NIV). This was God's purpose as well as the Servant's purpose. Steve Jeffery puts it this way: "The Servant consented to, and actively participated in, this ministry of sin-bearing and substitutionary death, in accordance with the will of God, to afflict him in the place of others."[11]

There was no provision in the Old Testament for one human being to suffer for the sins of another. But the many animal sacrifices simply could not be an adequate punishment for human sin. As if to underline this very thought, the Lord refers to him in verse 11 as "my righteous servant" (NIV). God loved Jesus' righteousness. In his very submission to the sufferings included in God's plan, Jesus delighted his Father. And yet the Father crushed him. That is *the* great mystery of our faith. In his love for us, God put his Son to grief. As profound as that mystery is the depth of God's love for us. These are the things that had "not been told" (52:15). They seem too good to be true. But they are true. The Servant gave himself, and God gave him, for our sins. He was pierced for our transgressions. "This is my blood of the covenant, which is poured out for many for the forgiveness of sins" (Matt. 26:28).

At this very simple meal today, you need not wonder whether Jesus' sufferings are adequate for the forgiveness of your sins. God is satisfied. Receive from his hand the signs of the new covenant: Jesus' body given and his blood shed. Believe.

HE SHALL BE SATISFIED
— *Isaiah 53:10–11* —

Was there a reason for Jesus' sufferings? The sufferings of Jesus Christ were supremely fruitful. Through the prophet, God promised that he would crown the suffering and death of his Son with massive bless-

---

11 Steve Jeffery, Michael Ovey, and Andrew Sach, *Pierced for Our Transgressions: Rediscovering the Glory of Penal Substitution* (Wheaton, IL: Crossway, 2007), 19.

ings for the world. The next chapter, Isaiah 54, describes those effects. Israel had become utterly barren, in exile, under the Lord's judgment. Nevertheless, Israel would begin to have children—many children. "'Sing, O barren one, who did not bear; break forth into singing and cry aloud, you who have not been in labor! For the children of the desolate one will be more than the children of her who is married,' says the LORD" (54:1). These are children born without labor pains. Where do they come from? They come from the "anguish" of the Servant. "He shall see his offspring. . . . Of the anguish of his soul he shall see . . ." (Isa. 53:10–11).[12] The Lord rewards his Servant with many children. In fact, there are so many that Israel's "tent" is much too small (54:2). Later in the chapter (54:13), the prophet promises that God's people will be instructed directly by him. In John's gospel, Jesus explained that this prophecy is fulfilled as the Father's teaching draws people to him by faith (John 6:45).

In the book of Acts, Paul and Barnabas reported to the church in Antioch how, through their preaching, God had "opened a door of faith to the Gentiles" (Acts 14:27). God was rewarding his Son by bringing new children into his people's tent. As you come to partake of Jesus' meal by faith today, you are part of the reward that God has given to Christ for the anguish of his soul. You are his delight today. "Me?" Yes, you. He saves you.

Then there is the promise that, for his people, God's "covenant of peace shall not be removed" (54:10). This peace with God arises from the punishment that the Servant bore: "Upon him was the chastisement that brought us peace, and with his wounds we are healed" (53:5). We cannot win this peace by our doing or suffering. Christ has gained it for us. "Since we have been justified by faith, we have peace with God through our Lord Jesus Christ" (Rom. 5:1).

There is a fourth element in chapter 54. Verse 17 says, "You will

---

12 Motyer, *The Prophecy of Isaiah*, 340.

refute every tongue that accuses you. This is the heritage of the servants of the LORD, and this is their vindication from me" (NIV). The inheritance of the people of God is the result of the anguish of the Servant. All that we have in possession was bought by his sufferings. We have a righteousness that comes from him. That is the result of the anguish of God's "righteous servant" (Isa. 53:11 NIV) as well. In his priestly work, taking our sins, our punishment, on himself, he also gives us his righteousness as an accounting. The joy that the Holy Spirit gives, revealing God's love for us, is just the beginning of the full inheritance (Rom. 5:5). On the last day, he will raise his own from the grave. Then the great results of his anguish will be fulfilled.

Many children, Jew and Gentile, born without human agency, taught by the Father of the saving power of his Son, have a settled peace with God and a righteous accounting before God. These arise from the anguish of Christ for us. This is the fruitfulness of the covenant fulfilled in the death and resurrection of Christ. How rich we are today on account of God's gracious plan! As you eat this bread, recognize that it is not the bread of sorrow but the nourishment of fellowship with this Christ. He sees the result of his sufferings, and he is satisfied today. As you drink the wine of his Table, entrust yourself to him again. Give thanks for the peace with God that protects you from all harm. As you eat and drink, rejoice that God has given you to his Son and that Christ delights in you as the fruit of the anguish of his soul.

CHAPTER FIVE

New Covenant Fulfillment

THE BREAD OF HEAVEN
— *John 6:54 (53–58)* —

In the desert, God sustained the lives of his people with manna, called "bread from heaven" (Ex. 16:4).[1] It was a matter of faith, but also of *survival.* Like they did, we depend on food to sustain us. As believers we depend on Christ to sustain and nourish us. The life that we share with him is eternal life. But we never receive it as a completed "thing," like an injection of medicine. We depend on *him* every day. Christ gives us life by the ministry of the Holy Spirit. That is what Jesus taught the crowds.

Notice how strong his statement is: "Truly, truly, I say to you, unless you eat the flesh of the Son of Man and drink his blood, you have no life in you" (v. 53). Feeding on him is essential to life.[2] In the next verse he says the same with the force of a guarantee: "Whoever feeds

---

1 Israel had grumbled in unbelief, but God cared for them.

2 D. A. Carson comments: "In first century Israel, bread was only one of two staples: again, eat bread, or die. In the same way, either Jesus dies and we live, or he does not die and we do. We must eat his flesh and drink his blood if we are to enjoy eternal life, or we cannot live. His death is substituted for our death. The way the extended metaphor of eating Jesus' flesh and drinking his blood remains powerful while avoiding any hint of cannibalism turns on the power of first century assumptions about food" ("Adumbrations of Atonement Theology in the Fourth Gospel," *Journal of the Evangelical Theological Society* 57, no. 3 [September 2014]: 516).

on my flesh and drinks my blood has eternal life, and I will raise him up on the last day" (v. 54). This eating and drinking are the indispensable and infallible guarantee of eternal life ("unless" and "whoever").

These unqualified statements lead to a certain conclusion: with the words "my flesh" and "my blood," Jesus did *not* refer to the Lord's Supper.[3] In fact, if Jesus had been speaking about the Lord's Supper, he would have contradicted himself. That is so because, just earlier in the synagogue discussion, Jesus assigns precisely the same benefits to *faith* that he ascribes to eating his flesh and drinking his blood in verse 54—eternal life and bodily resurrection: "This is the will of my Father, that everyone who looks on the Son and believes in him should have eternal life, and I will raise him up on the last day" (v. 40).

Clearly, not everyone who has eaten bread and drunk wine at the Table has been saved. And, conversely, not every person who has entered eternal glory has eaten and drunk at the Lord's Table. The dying thief who spoke with Jesus never sat at the Lord's Table, but he entered paradise that very day (Luke 23:43: "Truly, I say to you, today you will be with me in Paradise"). But we may *not* say the same thing about faith. Everyone who comes to Christ in faith has eternal life, as Jesus says explicitly: "Truly, truly, I say to you, whoever believes has eternal life" (v. 47; see also vv. 29, 35, 37, 39, 44).

What then did Jesus mean when he said, "Truly, truly, I say to you, unless you eat the flesh of the Son of Man and drink his blood, you have no life in you. Whoever feeds on my flesh and drinks my blood has eternal life, and I will raise him up on the last day" (vv. 53–54)? By these words Jesus was teaching that faith in him as crucified is the indispensable requirement of eternal life.[4] An important

---

3 At this point in his ministry, Jesus had not yet instituted the Lord's Supper. If he were now speaking about it, his synagogue hearers could not have understood these words.

4 He also calls it "abiding": his "abiding" in us, and ours in him (v. 56). Later in the gospel of John, Jesus speaks of our "abiding" in him, as he does here in 6:56—in his word and prayer (15:7), in his love (15:9, as the one who laid down his life for his friends, as in 6:51), and in obeying his commands (15:10–14).

clue to his meaning in verses 53–54 is that later in the passage he says that this "eating and drinking" will be possible only when the crucified Son of Man ascends to the Father and sends the life-giving Spirit (vv. 61–63).[5] He was speaking about the reality of which the Lord's Supper is a sign: saving union with him. Those who heard understood that without bread they would die. Either he would die, or they would die.

Earlier in the discussion, Jesus had spoken metaphorically of "the bread of life" (vv. 35, 48; see also vv. 32–33). He is the one whom the Father sent to give eternal life. His flesh, *given up to death*, is life giving (v. 51). It was "bread" in a way that Moses' manna, the type, could never be, because it could not give resurrection life.[6] Real and life-giving as manna was, it could not finally save from death. But Christ himself *will* raise us from death on the last day.

Then, in verses 35–40, Jesus speaks nonmetaphorically. The people were troubled, because they could not believe that Jesus had come down from heaven (v. 42). They knew his parents. But it was absolutely necessary for our salvation that the Word of God became flesh (see John 1:14). Only in this way could he give his life. "I am the living bread that came down from heaven. If anyone eats of this bread, he will live forever. And the bread that I will give for the life of the world is my flesh" (v. 51). A human being can live eternally only by the surrender to death of the flesh and blood of the Son of Man, and by believing, or "eating and drinking," of it. "By the Word and by faith, we enter into an intimate communion with Christ, such as the food a person eats, and the person who eats it."[7]

To press the point, Jesus went back to the metaphor and made

---

5 David G. Peterson, *Encountering God Together: Leading Worship Services That Honor God, Minister to His People, and Build His Church* (Phillipsburg, NJ: P&R Publishing, 2013), 170.

6 Resurrection life is "eternal life" in Jesus' speech here.

7 Herman Bavinck, *Reformed Dogmatics*, vol. 4, *Holy Spirit, Church, and New Creation*, ed. John Bolt, trans. John Vriend (Grand Rapids: Baker Academic, 2008), 567.

it stronger (v. 53, "So Jesus said . . ."). Only his flesh and blood save, and we must be joined to him. We return to where we began. It is Jesus Christ, now glorified, to whom we are joined by faith. By the Holy Spirit (vv. 62–63), Jesus sustains our life with his own, and will he raise us up on the last day. Of that, and of him, this meal assures us. John Calvin wrote, "He is now treating of the perpetual eating of faith. . . . There is nothing said here that is not figured and actually presented to believers in the Lord's Supper. Indeed, we might say that Christ intended the holy Supper to be a seal of this discourse."[8]

Take, eat, remember, and believe that the body and blood of our Lord Jesus Christ nourishes you to eternal life. Receive him once again in the power of his Spirit that he may strengthen and sustain you forever.

A RANSOM FOR MANY
— Mark 10:45 —

Jesus' disciples slowly came to recognize that he was the Christ. After Peter confessed this, Jesus set off to Jerusalem. He began to teach them about himself as the Son of Man and about what this meant for him. The title "Son of Man" came from the book of Daniel (7:13–14):

I saw in the night visions,

and behold, with the clouds of heaven
    there came one like a son of man,
and he came to the Ancient of Days
    and was presented before him.
And to him was given dominion

---

8 John Calvin, *The Gospel According to John, 1–10*, trans. T. H. L. Parker (Grand Rapids: Eerdmans, 1979), 170, quoted in Herman N. Ridderbos, *The Gospel of John: A Theological Commentary*, trans. John Vriend (Grand Rapids: Eerdmans, 1997), 237. Ridderbos notes several lines of argument, made by contemporary exegetes, that support Calvin's view.

and glory and a kingdom,
that all peoples, nations, and languages
    should serve him;
his dominion is an everlasting dominion,
    which shall not pass away,
and his kingdom one
    that shall not be destroyed.

"This is the one to whom the earth and its fullness belonged, and for whom the service of all nations was destined."[9] Daniel saw him receiving that glory. On the Mount of Transfiguration the disciples also saw a preview of Jesus' resurrection and exaltation glory (Mark 9:2–13; 2 Peter 1:16–18).

But there was another side to his teaching, a side not found in Daniel. Now he tells them clearly that, before his glorious reign, he will have to undergo a violent death.

> And taking the twelve again, he began to tell them what was to happen to him, saying, "See, we are going up to Jerusalem, and the Son of Man will be delivered over to the chief priests and the scribes, and they will condemn him to death and deliver him over to the Gentiles. And they will mock him and spit on him, and flog him and kill him. And after three days he will rise." (Mark 10:32–34)

Three times Jesus told them about his rejection and sufferings, each time more clearly (8:31; 9:31; 10:33–34). In response, Peter rebuked him (8:32), the disciples discussed who among them was greatest (9:34), and James and John asked for the places of honor in his glory (10:35–37). Was not the "Son of Man" a glorious king?

---

9 Geerhardus Vos, *Grace and Glory: Sermons Preached in the Chapel of Princeton Theological Seminary* (Edinburgh: Banner of Truth, 1994), 247–48.

What's all this about suffering? How could sufferings and glory fit together? They could not grasp it. Again, each time, Jesus stressed that his followers must be willing to suffer and serve.

The chapters reach their climax with James and John seeking the place of glory. Jesus rebukes them, asking, "Are you able to drink the cup that I drink, or to be baptized with the baptism with which I am baptized?" (10:38). Jesus uses Old Testament metaphors to ask whether these two are willing to suffer along with him. Sometimes the cup in the Old Testament refers to salvation. But more often it refers to the wrath of God's judgment on sin. Psalm 75:8 says, "For in the hand of the LORD there is a cup with foaming wine, well mixed, and he pours out from it, and all the wicked of the earth shall drain it down to the dregs" (see also Jer. 25:15–16). (The image of baptism is parallel to that of the cup.) Can James and John do this? They think so, but of course they cannot, not in the sense Jesus means. Still, he kindly says that they *will* join him in suffering.

The ten were indignant with James and John, so Jesus speaks to them all. Discipleship in the kingdom is not a matter of receiving power and prestige, but of becoming "slave of all" (10:44). Then he illustrates by presenting himself as example: "For even the Son of Man came not to be served but to serve, and to give his life as a ransom for many" (v. 45). The paradox that the *Son of Man* would give up his life as a ransom must have made Jesus' words like a thunderclap. But that kind of service defines discipleship in the kingdom.

Strange as it sounded, Jesus' offering his life as a "ransom for many" (literally, "in place of many"[10]) was something that he assumed as the given meaning of his whole life. Unlike them, and us, he had no goal of self-realization. Serving—indeed, giving up his life in the place of many—drove him, from his very appearance on the earth. He *came* to serve by way of offering his life as a ransom.

---

10 Leon Morris, *The Apostolic Preaching of the Cross*, 3rd rev. ed. (1965; repr., Grand Rapids: Eerdmans, 2000), 38.

For this reason the Father loves me, because I lay down my life
that I may take it up again. No one takes it from me, but I lay
it down of my own accord. I have authority to lay it down, and
I have authority to take it up again. This charge I have received
from my Father. (John 10:17–18)

He offered his life to God as a "ransom in place of many." A "ransom" is the price paid to free a slave. This bread and cup proclaim that
he has paid the ransom price for you. God has set you free from bondage to guilt and wrath. As you eat and drink today, remember that
you feast at the King's Table. By giving his life as a ransom, Christ has
given us the rule for living together: to *serve* each other. We cannot
atone for each other's sins. But, by the Spirit, we can imitate the love
and humility of the Son of Man. Now he has received the glory that
Daniel saw. Receive from Christ his body and blood, and follow him.

THE RANSOM PRICE
⏤ *Mark 10:45* ⏤

Why does Jesus refer to his death as a "ransom"? If "ransom" refers
to the price paid to free a slave, what was the condition of bondage
that cost Jesus his life? We find the answer by looking at a statement
that Jesus made earlier in Mark's gospel. In chapter 8, when he had
first explained the suffering that awaited him, you will remember that
Peter immediately objected. Jesus then warned him and the gathered
crowd of the danger of denying Jesus for the sake of acceptance by
people. Amid that warning, Jesus said,

For what does it profit a man to gain the whole world and
forfeit his soul? For what can a man give in return for his soul?
For whoever is ashamed of me and of my words in this adulterous and sinful generation, of him will the Son of Man also

be ashamed when he comes in the glory of his Father with the holy angels. (vv. 36–38)

Jesus refers to the hour of final judgment. At that hour, when the Lord declares a man's life forfeit and he faces eternal death, what can he give in exchange for his soul? If he were to have gained the approval of the whole world, or had received all the good things in the world, they would be completely useless. If a person were to offer these to God, writes Geerhardus Vos, "The offer would not be accepted, for a whole world cannot satisfy God. His justice demands neither gold, nor silver, but the soul, the spirit, the life of a man, because sin is a spiritual thing and it must be paid for in kind by the life of the sinner."[11]

The ransom is the price paid to God on judgment day for deliverance from eternal death. This is what Jesus had in mind when he said, "Even the Son of Man came not to be served but to serve, and to give his life a ransom for many" (Mark 10:45). Christ would pay, in judgment, for those whose lives are forfeit.

Here the price is life for life. Of course inanimate objects may not be substituted in the judgment of God. Our lives are lived before him: as his image, we are obligated to love and serve him. When we live in defiance of the covenant relationship, when we transgress his laws, he is offended because he is holy. Because sin is personal, punishment is personal, and thus the ransom must be personal.

But Jesus' life is more than any life. It is the life of the Son of Man. This is God's Son himself, the heir of creation, the Lord of life. This is the eternal fellow of his Father, the object of his Father's eternal delight. This is the Son, who with the Father and the Spirit freely planned to save a guilty people. This is the one who freely took on the task of paying the ransom price. Of course his life giving is adequate to satisfy divine justice and free us from the punishment it requires.

---

11 Vos, *Grace and Glory*, 251–52. Psalm 49:6–8 states that there is no ransom a person can pay to avoid death.

What did it cost Jesus to put himself in the place of guilty people, to receive their punishment? The sufferings of the perfect Son of God were very great, greater than we can imagine. And these he offered, not simply *for* people but *to* God, as the ransom price. How deeply precious his Son's sufferings were to God! "Christ redeemed us from the curse of the law by becoming a curse for us—for it is written, 'Cursed is everyone who is hanged on a tree'" (Gal. 3:13).

It was not only our need that moved Jesus to serve. It was the requirement of God's character and his election. This is something we can easily overlook in our self-centered world. It pleased God to save "many," because God loved. We cannot say why God has loved us this way. It was the pure, self-originating grace of God to save a people to belong to his Son. To fulfill the Father's plan was in Jesus' heart. To give his life was the only way to fulfill that plan.

Salvation, even eating and drinking the feast of the Lord's Table, is not finally for us. It is God's glory that is at the center of all life and history. He brings most glory to his Son by graciously saving the church. We had nothing to offer. Instead he gave his life as our ransom payment. Receive from Christ's hand the seal of his self-giving for you. Take, eat, remember, and believe that Christ gave himself as the ransom for your life.

ON THE NIGHT WHEN HE WAS BETRAYED
⸺ *1 Corinthians 11:23* ⸺

Judas betrayed Jesus into the hands of the priests, who had him crucified by the Romans. We are familiar with the story, and perhaps we have felt the distress of hearing Jesus say, "See . . . the Son of Man is betrayed into the hands of sinners" (Matt. 26:45).[12] Jesus certainly felt

---

12 In all the texts quoted here (except Luke 22:37; 1 Peter 1:18–20), the passive of παραδίδωμι (*paradídwmi*) describes either the acts of men (translated "betrayed"), or the act of the Father (translated "delivered up"), in delivering Jesus to death. Cf. Luke 22:19, "This is my body, which is given (διδόμενον, *didómenon*) for you."

the bitterness of Judas's betrayal, because he loved him. But as difficult as it is to understand, we are not to suppose that Jesus' betrayal to death was a surprise. Many times Jesus had forewarned his disciples of exactly this:

> See, we are going up to Jerusalem. And the Son of Man will be delivered over to the chief priests and scribes, and they will condemn him to death and deliver him over to the Gentiles to be mocked and flogged and crucified, and he will be raised on the third day. (Matt. 20:18–19; see also Matt. 17:22–23; 26:2; Mark 9:31; 10:33–34; Luke 18:32–33)

They had no idea what to make of these statements. The prediction of his suffering and death contradicted every expectation. But Jesus knew full well that it would happen, he knew why, and he embraced the reasons.

How did he know? He knew because it was foretold in the (Old Testament) Scriptures. Before his arrest, he warned the disciples: "I tell you that this Scripture must be fulfilled in me: 'And he was numbered with the transgressors.' For what is written about me has its fulfillment" (Luke 22:37, quoting Isa. 53:12). During his arrest, one of the disciples tried to protect Jesus from the soldiers. Jesus rebuked him: "How then should the Scriptures be fulfilled, that it must be so?" (Matt. 26:54). Jesus knew his prophecy of Isaiah: "The LORD has laid on him the iniquity of us all" (Isa. 53:6). It was God's purpose, revealed by the prophet, that his Servant, Jesus Christ, would be sacrificed for our sins.

Second, Jesus knew because he had embraced this mission, with his Father, in eternity. To understand the source of Jesus' death for us, we must go behind the Old Testament to its origin in God's eternal plan. We must never see Jesus' death as a merely human tragedy. After Jesus' resurrection, Peter preached, "This Jesus, delivered up according to the definite plan and foreknowledge of God, you crucified and killed by the hands of lawless men" (Acts 2:23). This is the great mystery: through the hands of wicked men, God purposed to accomplish exactly what happened, in order that we might be saved from our sins. God did this. So wrote Paul: "He was delivered up for our trespasses and raised for our justification" (Rom. 4:25). Behind the treachery of men was the holy, loving purpose of the Trinity.

Long after Pentecost, Peter wrote to Gentile believers in Asia Minor. Jesus' death

> ransomed [them] . . . not with perishable things such as silver
> or gold, but with the precious blood of Christ, like that of
> a lamb without blemish or spot. He was foreknown before
> the foundation of the world but was made manifest in the
> last times for the sake of you who through him are believers
> in God, who raised him from the dead and gave him glory.
> (1 Peter 1:18–21)[13]

It was God's plan "before the foundation of the world." Now it has been revealed. The Father and the Son had this in view, Peter writes, "for the sake of you."

When Paul would persuade suffering Roman believers that God constantly worked for their good, he brought forward the clincher: "He who did not spare his own Son but *gave him up for us all*, how will he not also with him graciously give us all things?" (Rom. 8:32). The Father gave him up.[14] No greater price could he pay.

If the betrayal had been unexpected, Jesus could not have said, "This is my body which is *for you*" (1 Cor. 11:24). But because his

---

13 Cf. 1 Peter 2:24.

14 Donald Macleod writes, of John 3:16 and Romans 8:32, "Both passages point to a priesthood of God the Father, 'giving' or 'giving up' his only Son" (Donald Macleod, *Christ Crucified: Understanding the Atonement* [Downers Grove, IL: InterVarsity Press, 2014], 25).

disciples could not grasp its meaning, Jesus gave them a meal, to seal on their minds that it was *for* them.[15] God's eternal love planned this and revealed it in the Scriptures. This is the love of your God for his people throughout the earth and across the ages. The Father, in love, delivered Christ up for your sins and raised him for your justification. Today he seals that love to your heart. Receive the bread and cup from his hands. Receive him. "Take, eat."

THE NEW COVENANT IN MY BLOOD
— *Luke 22:20* —

Despite God's faithfulness and patience, much of the Old Testament tells of the disobedience of the covenant people. When we read Israel's story, we might be inclined to say, "Most of what I see is unbelief and sin. Where was God's salvation?" There were always those in fellowship with the true God, and the prophets constantly urged Israel to faith and repentance. One of the most important prophetic promises was the inauguration of a "new covenant," in which God would bring about his saving purposes for his people. In Jeremiah 31:31–34, God promised to renew his exiled people, to write his law on their hearts, to forgive their sins, and to give them a true knowledge of himself. In other words, he would establish a relationship with his people that would bring salvation. Frustration, failure, and sin would yield to sovereign mercy.

The New Testament tells us that, through the cross, this new covenant has been set in motion. Jesus' identification of the cup at the Last Supper shows this. "This cup that is poured out for you is the new covenant in my blood" (Luke 22:20). Through his blood shed for us, we are reconciled to God, and the Holy Spirit has written his law on our hearts (2 Cor. 3:3). We know God truly. Under the

---

15 So Edmund P. Clowney, *The Church*, Contours of Biblical Theology, ed. Gerald Bray (Downers Grove, IL: InterVarsity Press, 1994), 289.

old covenant, believers trusted God's promises, but animal sacrifices could not remove guilt. (Just like this bread and cup, in themselves, cannot.)

Nonetheless, we need to be careful not to misunderstand the situation. Under the old covenant, believers received the same forgiveness that we do. David, for example, praises God for the clear conscience that God gave him by forgiving his sins:

> Blessed is the one whose transgression is forgiven,
> whose sin is covered.
> Blessed is the man against whom the LORD counts no iniquity,
> and in whose spirit there is no deceit.
>
> . . . .
>
> I acknowledged my sin to you,
> and I did not cover my iniquity;
> I said, "I will confess my transgressions to the LORD,"
> and you forgave the iniquity of my sin. (Ps. 32:1–2, 5)

Paul quotes Psalm 32 to show that God justifies the ungodly by faith (Rom. 4:5–8). David and, of course, Abraham before him were justified by faith.

Gracious as God's provision was, however, the sacrifices under the old covenant were only animals. Their repetition, year after year for centuries, showed that they could not atone for sin (Heb. 9:9; 10:2). There was no basis yet, in redemptive history, for justification.

With the sacrifice of Christ, everything has changed. If the animal sacrifices "cleansed" outwardly, states the writer to the Hebrews, "how much more will the blood of Christ, who through the eternal Spirit offered himself without blemish to God, purify our conscience from dead works to serve the living God" (Heb. 9:14). No animal could suffer the punishment for our sins, but Christ, the divine Son, did. Because of Christ's sacrifice and entrance into heaven, the writer urges, "Let us draw near with a true heart in full assurance of faith, with our hearts sprinkled clean from an evil conscience and our bodies washed with pure water" (10:22). The Old Testament believer, with a heart renewed by the Holy Spirit, trusted God's promise of forgiveness. David did. But he received forgiveness only because of what Jesus Christ finally *would* do many years later in history.

Jesus introduced the Supper so that we might look to him alone as the one who has accomplished our salvation. God's covenant with us is not based on our works. It is not based on animal sacrifices. The fellowship of salvation that we share with Christ is based on his all-sufficient sacrifice. God provided him, and gave him up, out of the depth of his love. The great promise of the new covenant is, "I will remember their sins and their lawless deeds no more" (Heb. 10:17, quoting Jer. 31:34). We need have no guilty conscience before our gracious God. His forgiveness is ours, and our conscience is free, now, to serve him. The Holy Spirit has written God's law on our hearts, and he continually strengthens us. In his grace, God is pleased with our service. Come boldly, receive these seals of his sacrifice, eat and drink, share today the fellowship of the new covenant, rejoice in the presence of Christ.

WHOM GOD PUT FORWARD
AS A PROPITIATION
— *Romans 3:21–26* —

When you think about the Lord's Table today, if you consider yourself unworthy to come into God's presence on account of sins, in a way you are correct. The apostle teaches that God's wrath is revealed against "all ungodliness and unrighteousness of men" (Rom. 1:18). Every single human being has the same problem. No one is righteous before God the judge. Jew and Gentile alike "are under sin" (3:9). On the last day, when God utters his judgment, every mouth will be silent. There is simply none who is righteous (3:19–20). The law given to Israel was good, but it provided no way for a person to be justified (v. 20). The old covenant was not able to provide a righteousness for God's people that could stand in his judgment. Thus, all face his wrath. We all have some sense of it.

But Paul teaches that now "the righteousness of God," *from* God, has been revealed (v. 21). It does not come to us by law keeping. It is given as a gift to those who believe. It is "through faith in Jesus Christ" (v. 22). It is available to all who entrust themselves to him.[16] God has provided righteousness for every believer. Paul states it this way: "All are justified by his grace as a gift, through the redemption that is in Christ Jesus, whom God put forward as a propitiation" (vv. 24–25).[17]

There are three elements to his statement. First, justification: believers, who cannot be found righteous on account of their own behavior (they are completely guilty if judged that way), are declared righteous by God. Their guilt is no longer counted against them. The Westminster Shorter Catechism puts it this way: "Justification is an act of God's free grace, wherein he pardoneth all our sins, and accepteth us as righteous in his sight, only for the righteousness of Jesus Christ imputed to us, and received by faith alone."[18] What motivated God to

---

16 Despite recent disagreement, the traditional view, which reads πίστεως Ἰησοῦ Χριστοῦ (*pisteōs Iēsou Christou*) as an objective genitive, "faith in Jesus Christ," is exegetically persuasive. D. A. Carson makes a strong case for this in "Atonement in Romans 3:21–26," in *The Glory of the Atonement: Biblical, Historical and Practical Perspectives; Essays in Honor of Roger Nicole*, ed. Charles E. Hill and Frank A. James III (Downers Grove, IL: InterVarsity Press, 2004), 126. This meditation is based on Carson's exegesis.

17 Donald Macleod (along with Calvin) makes a compelling case that ἱλαστήριον (*hilastērion*) in verse 25 refers to the covering of sin by sacrificial blood on the Day of Atonement, now climactically fulfilled by Christ's shed blood. In contrast to the way it is sometimes put, the notion of "covering sin" is not an alternative to "propitiation" but is essential to it. "God can be propitiated only if sin is expiated; and sin is expiated only in order that God be propitiated" (*Christ Crucified*, 110–16, 136–46). Carson agrees with this conclusion in "Atonement in Romans 3:21–26," 130.

18 Question and answer 33.

provide this free pardon of guilt? It was "by his grace as a gift" (v. 24). His deepest motive was his own gracious purpose. This is our God!

Second, Paul tells us the means of justification in history: "through the redemption that is in Christ Jesus" (v. 24), or that "came by Christ Jesus" (NIV). God liberated his people Israel from their captivity to Egypt and from their exile in Babylon. That was a picture of what he has now done finally "by Christ Jesus." "Redemption" involves the payment of a ransom price. Paul is saying that Jesus' death was the price paid, which frees us from the penalty of death. In other words, God has acted to free us from the penalty that he himself required.

Justification has come through redemption. But now, third, Paul goes further to tell us the means by which this redemption was accomplished. Christ was, by God, "put forward as a propitiation" (v. 25). A "propitiation" is a sacrifice that turns away wrath. In Israel's worship, the word translated "propitiation" referred to the place, in the Holy of Holies, for the sprinkling of the sacrificial animal's blood on the Day of Atonement (see Heb. 9:5). The blood was sprinkled on the covering of the ark, under which were the tablets of the (broken) law. God transacted forgiving mercy toward his people because the blood covered, or removed, their sin.

But the very repetition of these sacrifices, year after year, for centuries, signaled that they were inadequate. Paul is saying that Christ's sacrifice on the cross actually *accomplished* this propitiation. What the symbol suggested has now been done, and God himself has "put it forward," or made this known, to all. God's righteous wrath for sin is the universal human problem. But now he has made his Son a "propitiation by his blood" (v. 25) and thus turned his wrath away. God has revealed this; he offers this.

How then do we accept this gift? The last words of verse 25 explain it: "to be received by faith." Faith in Christ, as the propitiation put forward by God, receives God's righteousness and pardon. God has provided him for the guilt of Jew and Gentile.

We have no claim on this righteousness, as if it were a reward. No, it is God's free gift at the cost of Christ's blood. We do not receive it as good people, but as guilty people who entrust ourselves to him. But we have another amazing thought presented by the apostle. God is both "just" and "the justifier." His personal righteousness, his integrity, remains absolute. His justice is not diminished by the cross but *proclaimed* by it. Christ was set forth as a propitiation, that God might be evidently righteous. Before the day of Christ's death, not once was the full penalty for sin paid. Never were the demands of God's holy justice satisfied, even for Old Testament believers.[19] God was "forbearing" (v. 25). But now his justice is vindicated, because its penalty has been fully paid and his wrath turned away.

God required a full satisfaction. God provided a full satisfaction. Now these sins must be pardoned. Our conscience requires nothing less than this, for our guilt is real. Our God provided the redemption in Christ Jesus. This is why Jesus referred to the wine as "my blood of the covenant, which is poured out for many for the forgiveness of sins" (Matt. 26:28).

Now receive this seal of his sacrifice again. Take, eat, remember, and believe. Accept it as those who have been fully pardoned through his blood. Receive it because you have received the righteousness of God.

God Reconciled Us to Himself
— *2 Corinthians 5:19–21* —

Why did Christ die? We may think of Jesus' own goal—to save. We may think of his enemies—the Jewish and Roman leaders and their murderous envy. We may think of his heart—the love that he bears toward the world. We may say, with Paul, "The Son of God . . . loved

---

19 Macleod writes, "It is clear from Romans 3:25 that the cross cast its effect before it, justifying God in forgiving sins he had forgiven millennia ago" (*Christ Crucified*, 134).

me and gave himself for me" (Gal. 2:20). All these are "why." But Paul tells us that the *Father* is the source of the reconciliation accomplished for us. He reconciled the world (2 Cor. 5:19); he publishes this message through us; he appeals to us to receive the reconciliation (v. 20). It was not only Jesus' intention to reconcile us to God; it was the Father's intention to reconcile us to himself. The cross of Christ was the work of the one God, in perfect unity of intention and accomplishment. God is our Savior—Father, Son, and Holy Spirit.[20]

The apostle Paul urges us to be reconciled to God. How does this reconciliation take place? Reconciliation is not just a change in outlook or feeling. It is based on something that happened in history. There had to be something done, Paul writes, to change the situation between God and us before we could be brought together. God did it "in Christ." The word translated "reconciled" conveys that a change took place. In short, our sin was imputed to Christ, and his righteousness was imputed to us. "Impute" means to "count" or to "reckon." In verse 21, Paul sums up his message this way: "He made him to be sin who knew no sin, so that in him we might become the righteousness of God."

Verse 19 says, "God was reconciling the world to himself, not counting their trespasses against them." Our "trespasses" are the record of broken commandments. God could not be our friend as long as these trespasses remained on our record. Through Christ, our trespasses are not counted against us. God did not ignore them. But, because of the cross, God does not count them against us anymore. God accomplished the entire reconciliation. Just before he died, Jesus cried, "It is finished" (John 19:30). He meant that his sufferings were

---

20 See Sinclair B. Ferguson, "Preaching the Atonement," in Hill and James, *Glory of the Atonement*, 430. Pierre Charles Marcel writes beautifully of God our Savior: "The *Father* who takes pity on me; who abased Himself for me in *his Son*; and who lives in me by *his Holy Spirit*: God *for* me, God *with* me, and God *in* me" (*In God's School: Foundations for a Christian Life*, trans. Howard Griffith [Eugene, OR: Wipf & Stock, 2009], 23, italics his).

complete. God "made him to be sin" for us (2 Cor. 5:21). Paul refers to this event as, literally, "the reconciliation" (v. 19). It is a definite, accomplished event. This is the good news that we receive by faith.

And we should notice too that the exchange happens both ways. "In him," we have become "the righteousness of God" (v. 21). Again this phrase refers to the obedience of Jesus Christ, as God assessed it. He was perfect, spotless—he delighted to do the will of his Father all his life. God testified his pleasure with Christ at his baptism in the Jordan: "This is my beloved Son, with whom I am well pleased" (Matt. 3:17). Again at his transfiguration on the mountain, the Father said, "This is my beloved Son, with whom I am well pleased; listen to him" (Matt. 17:5). Jesus' obedience extended to the very point of his death (Phil. 2:8). His sufferings were real as he willingly submitted to the Father's will to save us. Then, at last, when he raised him from death in the resurrection itself, the Father declared his satisfaction with the whole of Christ's obedient life. That is what Paul means by "the righteousness of God," which *we* are counted when we are united to Christ. My sins are not counted against me, but counted against Christ; his righteousness is counted freely to me. Now, it is clear that God is reconciled. We do not become so inwardly good that God can overlook our sins. The truth is much, much greater! Rather, we have Jesus' perfect righteousness counted as ours, and God does not count our sins against us anymore. Christ did this for us. The Father did this for us in Christ. This is the love of our God for us. This love drives us, all of us for whom Christ died, to live for him (2 Cor. 5:14–15). It is on account of him that we are now part of the "new creation" (2 Cor. 5:17).

The Father is not estranged from or "cool" toward us. The Father has reconciled us to himself. Communion with him is as close as it can be. When Christ is mine, all that is his belongs to me as well. One with him, this bread is his body. This cup is the new covenant in his blood. Eat, drink, rejoice, and thank God that he has reconciled you in Christ.

CHAPTER SIX

The Riches of Union with Christ

TAKE, EAT, DRINK
— *1 Corinthians 1:30* —

At the Last Supper, Jesus took bread in his hands. He then gave it the significance of his body "given" over to death. He took the cup of wine used in the Passover and gave it the meaning of his blood, shed for us. He knew that God called him to lay down his life as a sacrifice for our sins. But when he gave the bread and the cup this meaning, he did not leave it there, as though his disciples might simply *watch* what he did. He told them to *receive* the bread and cup, to take it, to eat it, to drink it. In other words, he founded "a meal in which the disciples consume his body and blood and so enter into the most intimate communion with him."[1]

The good news of salvation is that God has provided everything for us in his Son. The Corinthian church was divided because people were self-impressed with distinctive achievements and knowledge. But the apostle called them to humility by recognizing that their true distinction was to have been loved and set apart by God's grace. Only

---

1 Herman Bavinck, *Reformed Dogmatics*, vol. 4, *Holy Spirit, Church, and New Creation*, ed. John Bolt, trans. John Vriend (Grand Rapids: Baker Academic, 2008), 567.

Christ was their true "wisdom." Paul wrote of God's choice, "because of him you are in Christ Jesus, who became to us wisdom from God." Paul then elaborates the "wisdom" that Christ is, in three things: "righteousness and sanctification and redemption" (1 Cor. 1:30).

As sinners, we need a righteousness that can stand in God's judgment. God has provided that righteousness in the resurrected Christ. As people inclined to break God's laws, to sin, we need to be "sanctified"—made holy in heart and life. God has provided that holiness in the resurrected Christ. As captives to the world and its ways of rebellion and death, we need to be freed from its power. God has provided that in his death and resurrection. Of course, our need is total. If we do not have the whole Christ, we have no Christ, because our need is pervasive. But we do have the whole Christ, in all that he has done.

We are not saved by receiving something *from* Christ, but by receiving Christ himself, by faith. In the gospel, God sets out the crucified and resurrected Christ as the source of life, and he calls to all, "Receive him!" In the Last Supper, Jesus was doing exactly the same thing. This is why Christ commanded his disciples "take, eat," and "drink of it, all of you" (Matt. 26:26–27). This is his instruction to us.

Take and eat his body. Drink his blood. As you do, you say, as it were, "I have displeased the Father, I deserve death, but I receive you as righteousness, that I may be found righteous." You say, "I receive your crucified body and shed blood that I may be counted forgiven." And the Father says to you, "Your sins are forgiven for his name's sake" (1 John 2:12).

Eat his body and drink the cup of the new covenant. As you do, you say to Christ, "I receive you as sanctification that I may live a holy life. Enable me, in your power, to 'put to death the deeds of the body'" (Rom. 8:13). Christ says to you, "At one time you were darkness, but now you are light in the Lord. Walk as children of light" (Eph. 5:8).

As you eat this bread and drink the cup of the Lord, you say, "You are the one who, by your blood, has freed me from captivity to sin

and to the twisted norms of this world. I receive you as my Savior."
The Lord says, in turn, to you, "Christ redeemed us from the curse of
the law by becoming a curse for us. . . . Do not submit again to a yoke
of slavery" (Gal. 3:13; 5:1).

Christ gave himself for us, and he gives himself to us. From him, life
flows forth into our souls. The Father delights that you should receive
all you need by union with Christ. Eat, drink, and believe that, because
of God, Christ is your righteousness, sanctification, and redemption.

RIGHTEOUS IN CHRIST
— *Romans 4:5* —

We have sinned against God. We cannot earn his favor. How then can
God justify us? How can God look at our lives and acquit us of guilt?
How can it be true that "there is . . . now *no* condemnation for those
who are in Christ Jesus" (Rom. 8:1)? God does not play favorites. He
does not compromise truth (even about believers!) in order to reach a
"desired" conclusion. He is, after all, righteous. He is never guilty of
a false judgment.

Certainly there is no good that we can do to cover the guilt of our
sins. Even if we could live perfectly, which we surely cannot, the past
would remain. We are not what we "wish we had been." We are our
lives, nothing more. God knows this and he always judges truthfully.

Thank God, the apostle answers our question: "To the one who
does not work but believes in him who justifies the ungodly, his faith
is counted as righteousness" (Rom. 4:5). According to the norm of
God's law, this person is "ungodly." God does not ground his judgment on goodness found in this person. We may not feel comfortable
labeling someone as "ungodly," but God has authority to judge. "Ungodly" is this person's character. God's law says that he is displeasing
to God. Again, then, how can God justify him? He justifies him by
grace, as a gift. And he does so without in any way compromising his

righteousness. He is "just and the justifier of the one who has faith in Jesus" (Rom. 3:26).

There is a righteousness that God counts as belonging to the one who has faith. It is not the faith itself. Our faith, no matter how strong, is never a perfect thing. One man said, "I believe; help my unbelief!" (Mark 9:24). That will always be the truth about each of us in this life. Faith cannot be my righteousness. Why does Paul write about faith then? He writes about it because faith is just receiving the righteousness of God, given as a gift. "That is why it depends on faith, in order that the promise may rest on grace," he says in Romans 4:16. If it were the moral value of faith that took the place of righteousness in God's judgment, faith would be a "good work." The apostle will have none of that. He is adamant that justification comes to "the one who does *not* work but believes" (cf. also Rom. 3:20–28; 4:4; Gal. 2:16). When it comes to justification, faith has no content of its own. We simply receive and rest in the righteous Christ, given as a gift. God pronounces ungodly believers "righteous" because he counts Christ's righteousness as belonging to them. That pronouncement is permanent and unchangeable.

Receive these tokens of Christ as receiving Christ again. He is yours and you are his. And the Spirit will seal to you again that God finds you righteous in Christ.

THE SECOND ADAM
— Romans 5:17 —

In Romans 5, Paul writes, "If, because of one man's trespass, death reigned through that one man, much more will those who receive the abundance of grace and the free gift of righteousness reign in life through the one man Jesus Christ" (v. 17). Righteousness is a "free gift." Because he represented us, Adam's sin implicated us all. So God freely provided a second "Adam," Jesus Christ, to represent us. God counts his righteousness as belonging to us.

Therefore, as one trespass led to condemnation for all men, so one act of righteousness leads to justification and life for all men. For as by the one man's disobedience the many were made sinners, so by the one man's obedience, the many will be made righteous. (vv. 18–19)

The "all" and the "many" are those who, by faith, "receive . . . the free gift," as Paul says in verse 17. The "one act of righteousness" and "the one man's obedience" are phrases that express God's evaluation of the whole life of Jesus Christ.

This righteousness of Christ is perfect and adequate. It is a whole, not pieced together bit by bit, but it is the perfect obedience of God's Son, culminating in his death for us (see Phil. 2:8: he became "obedient to the point of death, even death on a cross"). That obedience satisfied the righteous demands of God's law. For it, God raised Christ and exalted him to the highest place in his ascension to glory (Phil. 2:9). God provided this for us. It requires no completion or addition. The entire righteousness that we need is outside us, in Christ Jesus. You have either all of it or none of it, because either you have Christ or you do not.[2] As a believer, Paul no longer lived like a Pharisee. Rather, he was confident that he would "be found in him [Christ], not having a righteousness of my own that comes from the law, but that which comes through faith in Christ, the righteousness from God for faith" (Phil. 3:9).[3]

When God gives us Christ, out of free grace (without any merit on our part), he also freely justifies us. We are free of guilt and punishment, and we have eternal life. Eat this bread and drink the cup, and let God confirm your faith that, as God has promised, you have received his righteousness. You received the sign and seal of it in baptism. By

---

2 See Herman Bavinck, *Our Reasonable Faith*, trans. Henry Zylstra (Grand Rapids: Eerdmans, 1956), 453–54.

3 My translation.

this bread and cup, Christ assures you of this righteousness by personally giving you his body and blood.

THE FATHER'S FREE FORGIVENESS
― Romans 4:6–8 ―

In the psalm of David, Paul read about God's free forgiveness. God counted righteousness to David "apart from works" (Rom. 4:6). David had sinned quite seriously, and, when he was brought to admit it to God, he knew God's blessing once more. That is his reflection in Psalm 32:1–2, quoted in Rom. 4:7–8: "Blessed are those whose lawless deeds are forgiven, and whose sins are covered; blessed is the man against whom the Lord will not count his sin."

It is a fact that, when we are united to Christ, God justifies us. That includes counting Christ's righteousness as ours and forgiving all our sins. Free justification of the ungodly, apart from what we do, is absolutely wonderful. It means that we can never again lose Christ and that God will never condemn us. "There is . . . now no condemnation for those who are in Christ Jesus" (Rom. 8:1). Believers are those, as David wrote, "against whom the Lord will not count his sin" (4:8). God remains always for us (8:31–34). Christ—the righteous, resurrected one—intercedes effectively for us, and God does not reverse the imputation of Christ's righteousness.

However, justification does *not* mean that we will no longer commit sins, even serious sins. It certainly does not imply that God is pleased with us when we sin. (Our sins still deserve punishment and, if we were not in Christ, would bring punishment.)

We can "grieve the Holy Spirit" (Eph. 4:30; see also Gen. 6:6). The Westminster Confession of Faith, 11.5, describes this reality of the covenant of grace this way: "God doth continue to forgive the sins of those that are justified; and, although they can never fall from the state of justification, yet they may, by their sins, fall under God's fatherly displeasure, and not have the light of His countenance restored unto them, until they humble themselves, confess their sins, beg pardon, and renew their faith and repentance."

John Calvin says that, while God does not cease to love his children, he is "wondrously angry" with them. He shows this not out of hatred but out of love, to stir us up to obedience.[4] He loves us too well not to set us straight (Heb. 12:7–10).

Thus, Jesus teaches us to pray, "Forgive us our debts, as we also have forgiven our debtors" (Matt. 6:12). John writes, "If we confess our sins, he is faithful and just to forgive us our sins and to cleanse us from all unrighteousness" (1 John 1:9); and "If anyone does sin, we have an advocate with the Father, Jesus Christ the righteous. He is the propitiation for our sins, and not for ours only but also for the sins of the whole world" (1 John 2:1–2).

Christ's righteousness, though it is "outside" of us (it is his, not ours), is not like a bank deposit, which we can draw upon when we get into moral debt with God. Christ is a person, and our relation to him is personal. Justification is an act grounded on our union, by faith, with the righteous, resurrected Christ. That union is unbreakable, because the Holy Spirit will never leave us. Hence we do not gain, then lose, and then regain forgiveness. When we sin, our union with Christ is not broken.

However, our *communion* with Christ may be. Our sins bring displeasure to God. When we sin, we rightly have a sense of guilt, pain, and alienation. Our assurance of God's love weakens, and conscience loses its peace. This is not simply fallen pride; it is not abnormal or pathological for believers to react this way. We are in a

---

4 Calvin, *Inst.*, 1:557 (3/2.12), quoted in Kevin DeYoung, *The Hole in Our Holiness: Filling the Gap between Gospel Passion and the Pursuit of Godliness* (Wheaton, IL: Crossway, 2012), 74.

relationship with the living Christ. If you are married, you should not expect smiles and laughter when you insult your spouse. Our relationship with God is no less personal, even though it is more certain. We are wounded by the sense of guilt, and we wish to restore communion with him. No child wishes to remain under his father's frown.[5]

When we displease God, he wants us to repent. When we repent, there is joy in heaven (Luke 15:7)! Jesus tells us to confess our sins to the Father, to ask forgiveness every day (Matt. 6:12). John says to confess our "sins"—not a general unworthiness, but "sins" (in the plural), specific offenses against God (1 John 1:9). He loves us. We do not wish him to be unhappy with us. So we are to confess our sins and turn from them (repent of them). It is not despair but faith that moves us so to pray. We may well need to make confession to people as well. This is equally important in our relationship with God. We ask, and the promise is that he, in his righteousness, forgives. He does this because he has already accepted us in Christ, "the propitiation" for our sins (1 John 2:1–2). He is already our Father.

Self-humbling, confession, and prayer are the way in which God strengthens assurance of his free justification. God uses them to strengthen our consciousness of his grace and forgiveness. But we must ask. So, as you come to the Table today, come with a humble heart. Resolve before God to clear your conscience and to keep it clear, by the blood of Christ. Know that Jesus gives you the very signs of his sacrifice, his body and blood shed for the forgiveness of sins.

---

5 It is equally true that our obedience gives God pleasure. His grace and love of benevolence for the elect does not change. But his love of delight does. And as Paul says, as a model for every believer, "We make it our aim to please him" (2 Cor. 5:9). For discussion of the distinction between God's love of benevolence and his love of delight, see Francis Turretin, *Institutes of Elenctic Theology*, vol. 1, *First through Tenth Topics*, trans. George Musgrave Giger, ed. James T. Dennison Jr. (Phillipsburg, NJ: P&R Publishing, 1992), 242.

And receive the assurance that your sins will never stand between you and the Father, because he has accepted you in Christ.

FREED FROM SIN'S POWER
⁓ *Romans 6:11* ⁓

As Paul explained the gospel to the church in Rome, he had to answer the kind of question that might have been raised in the synagogue: "Are we to continue in sin that grace may abound?" (Rom. 6:1). After his discussion of God's overflowing, justifying grace, in the previous chapter of Romans, this is a natural question. If justification is by grace alone, through faith alone, by the righteousness of Christ alone, why not sin as much as . . . ? One might draw this inference. It is a serious question.

Paul answers sharply: No! Believers are the kind of people who simply cannot live this way. Why not? Because believers are no longer under the power of sin. "We, who are the kind of people who have died to sin, how can we still live in it?" (v. 2).[6] In the next verses (vv. 3–5), he gives the basis for that claim. Water baptism signifies and seals something real about each believer: he has been united to Christ, the Christ who died and now has been raised. Each believer in his union with Christ shares Christ's death and resurrection already. (Baptism does not create this union, but it does make it visible symbolically.) This is an experiential reality for each Christian: "We have been united with him in a death like his" (v. 5); "our old self was crucified with him in order that the body of sin might be brought to

---

6 Dr. Sinclair B. Ferguson suggested this translation in "The Reformed View," *Christian Spirituality: Five Views of Sanctification*, ed. Donald L. Alexander (Downers Grove, IL: InterVarsity Press, 1988), 57. Cf. Douglas J. Moo's comment, "The indefinite pronoun οἵτινες is often equivalent in the NT to the simple relative pronoun ὅς), but it is used deliberately here with a 'qualitative' nuance" (*The Epistle to the Romans*, The New International Commentary on the New Testament, ed. Gordon D. Fee [Grand Rapids: Eerdmans, 1996], 357n24).

nothing, so that we would no longer be enslaved to sin" (v. 6); "one who has died has been set free from sin" (v. 7)[7]; "if we have died with Christ, we believe that we will also live with him" (v. 8)—death to sin with Christ, resurrection life with Christ.

What has happened for us is grounded in what happened to Christ. What is true of the believer was true *first* for Christ himself. Now, as raised from death, Christ will never die again. Death has no power over him. Paul puts the sharp point on this by referring to Christ's death as "once for all" (v. 10). Since he was the sinless one, there was no requirement for his death except his bearing our sins.[8] He died, under the power of sin, because he was our substitute. But that could take place only once and never be repeated. God raised him. How could he ever die again? It is unthinkable.

In verse 11, Paul draws this conclusion for us: "So you also must *consider yourselves* dead to sin and alive to God in Christ Jesus." The link that Paul places between verse 10 and verse 11 is strong. It is "so also."[9] In other words, there is a strong parallel between Christ and believers: Christ's death to sin was "once for all," so also believers' death to sin's power was "once for all." His resurrection, "life to God," is "once for all," so also believers are alive to God "once for all" (and from now on). Sin is not the lord of our lives anymore. It cannot be,

---

7 Greek: "has been justified from sin" (see note on Romans 6:7 in ESV). In this context, the use of the verb δικαιόω (*dikaiō*) means "to set free," not "to declare righteous." I draw this conclusion because "sin" is in view in this chapter as a "controlling lord" or a "dominating power." In other words, Paul is addressing not the guilt of sin but the power of sin over life. Cf. verse 6, δουλεύειν (*douleuein*), "to serve as a slave," and verse 9, κυριεύω (*kurieuō*), "to dominate"; and notice sinners are described as "enslaved" in verses 12, 14, 16. See also Moo, *Epistle to the Romans*, 376–77. For further reading on this freedom, luminously named "definitive sanctification" by John Murray, see his *Collected Writings of John Murray*, vol. 2, *Systematic Theology*, ed. Iain H. Murray (Edinburgh: Bannner of Truth, 1977), 277–93; Richard B. Gaffin Jr., *By Faith, Not by Sight: Paul and the Order of Salvation*, 2nd ed. (Phillipsburg, NJ: P&R Publishing, 2013), 77–85.

8 Bearing sin was the entire rationale of his death. "Christ died for our sins in accordance with the Scriptures" (1 Cor. 15:3).

9 οὕτως καὶ (*houtōs kai*, "therefore").

because we are one with the resurrected Lord Jesus. This is not wishful thinking. This is God's Word about us as believers. God is telling us our identity in Christ. We are to believe it and obey God on the basis of it. Alongside free forgiveness, freedom from the power of sin is a "twin" gift for every believer, purchased with Christ's blood.

There is more to say, of course. In verses 12 and following, the apostle urges believers not to offer their bodies any longer as slaves to sin. Though in "the inner man" we are alive with resurrection life, in the "outer man" (the "mortal body" with "its passions")[10] we still need to exercise the power of the Spirit to put sin to death (see also 8:13). But the fact of our union with Christ means that, just as Christ has died to sin, we have too. In the deepest part of our humanity, we have made a definitive break with the power of sin. We are alive with Christ's life. We are no longer "dead" in trespasses and sins (Eph. 2:1). God has made us "alive together with Christ" (Eph. 2:5–6). All this is the reason that Paul so emphatically says "no!" to the proposal that we may live in sin in order that grace might increase. It is simply impossible, because the One with whom we are united "lives to God." Sin will not be—is not—our master, because we are under the grace of God (v. 14).

All this was signified in your baptism. At a basic level it is also signified at this Table. Eating Christ's body and drinking his blood are God's signs of our union with him. His blood atoned for us and his life is given to us. Here we need to look away from our experiences, however we think of them, and look instead to heaven, where our Lord Christ is. He has given us the Spirit of life. Whatever the power of sin may seem to be in your experience, there is a deeper reality about you. God has freed you from that enslaving master. Christ is your Lord and your life. Entrust yourself and all your days to the Lord Jesus Christ and "present yourselves to God as those who have been

---

10 See also Paul's use of this contrast in 2 Corinthians 4:16: "Though our outer self is wasting away, our inner self his being renewed day by day."

brought from death to life" (v. 13). Eat and drink in the confidence of the power of the Christ who dwells in you.

AT THE FATHER'S TABLE
— *Romans 8:15–16* —

As believers we have the freedom and privilege of God's children. The greatest of these is the ministry of the Holy Spirit. John Calvin wrote that the Spirit's most important ministry is to assure us of our adoption (Rom. 8:15–16). Nothing we did, or could do, led God to bring us into his family. It was his grace alone, granted to us before the creation of the world (vv. 29–30). As the Spirit persuades us of God's grace, we are able to unburden our hearts, crying out, "Abba! Father!"

We can obey God as children because we trust him. Calvin picks up Paul's contrast in verse 15 between "slaves," with their "fear," and "sons."[11] Servants are afraid of the slightest failure. Their masters are very particular and harsh. But children, who know a father's kindness, gladly bring him their "projects," even with their defects. Why? Because they know that their dad accepts them and will not point out their flaws. He loves the attempt, because he loves his child. That is true of our heavenly Father. He loves us, so he loves and accepts our obedience. Scripture teaches that God is pleased with his children: presenting our bodies as a living sacrifice pleases God (Rom. 12:1), protecting the weaker brother pleases God (Rom. 14:13–18), faith pleases God (Heb. 11:6), sharing with others pleases God (Heb. 13:16), keeping God's commands pleases him (1 John 3:22).[12] God wants us to trust him. It is the Spirit's ministry to reassure us that God accepts us as his dear children.

We are his children because we are one with his dear Son. Receive Christ again today, in this bread and wine, that you may know the

---

11 Calvin, *Inst.*, 1:837 (3/19.5).
12 Cf. DeYoung, *Hole in Our Holiness*, 69.

assurance of his Spirit. The Christ at God's right hand lives in you by his Spirit. He strengthens you to offer your life as a sacrifice of love to the Father.

ADOPTED FOREVER
— *Romans 8:13* —

The Spirit leads us to live for the Father's pleasure. He leads us to "put to death the deeds of the body" (Rom. 8:13). We need this help, of course, because we are still in the body. We are engaged in warfare. At the Jordan River, the Father poured out the Spirit on Jesus to strengthen him for his ministry as Savior. Jesus had no inclination to sin. He did not have any "deeds of the body," like we do.[13] He was God's eternal Son, God the Son, while we are adopted sons. But because of his true humanity, he had all the temptations that arise from the weakness of being human. A basic part of his humiliation was having to "undergo the miseries of this life," and being exposed to "the indignities of the world," "the infirmities in his flesh," and "the temptations of Satan."[14] Our Lord needed the Spirit's ministry to persevere in God's call to obedience.[15] The Spirit was his constant companion. He strengthened Jesus in his obedience to the Father— obedience, Paul tells us, that was "to the point of death, even death on a cross" (Phil. 2:8).

In Romans 8:17, Paul writes, "if children, then heirs—heirs of God and fellow heirs with Christ, provided we suffer with him in order that we may also be glorified with him." Then he goes on to

---

13 He is "holy, innocent, unstained, separated from sinners, and exalted above the heavens" (Heb. 7:26).

14 See Westminster Shorter Catechism, question and answer 27, and Westminster Larger Catechism, question and answer 48.

15 Luke tells us that Jesus was led by the Spirit in his great temptations in the wilderness, when Satan tempted him to disbelieve his unique sonship (Luke 4:1–13). Later, we read that Jesus "rejoiced in the Holy Spirit" when he learned of the disciples' ministry (Luke 10:21).

write about "the sufferings of this present time" (v. 18). The creation has been subjected to God's curse on sin, the "futility" of death (vv. 20–21). The whole creation groans for release. Believers groan for release; and the Spirit, too, groans within us for release from this futility. When will that come? It will come with "the redemption of our bodies" (v. 23), when Christ returns. We are sons now, but then God will reveal this to the whole creation by raising our bodies. Along with the whole creation, we will share Christ's resurrection glory. With him we will inherit the earth.

Until then, the Spirit gives us strength to continue in prayer, in faith, in obedience. In our sufferings we have the fellowship of the risen Christ. Remember, today, that in order to give us that fellowship, God "did not spare his own Son but gave him up for us all" on the cross (v. 32). That was, and it remains, the love of God for us. Nothing in all creation can separate us from the love of God in Christ Jesus our Lord.

At this Table, Christ gives you graphic signs of his communion, signs of the communion that you enjoy with him. He feeds you. He will sustain you until your faith is turned to sight. Take, eat, remember, and believe that Christ nourishes you with himself until the day he will raise you from the dead.

FORGIVENESS FROM THE HEART
— *Matthew 18:21–22* —

Jesus' teaching about going to be reconciled with a brother (Matt. 18:15–20) prompts Peter to ask: "Lord, how often will my brother sin against me, and I forgive him? As many as seven times?" (v. 21). That is a great question. We may put it this way: how forgiving does God require us to be? Jesus' answer, "not . . . seven times, but seventy-seven times" (v. 22), shows how radical his grace is. We are to continue to forgive over and over. There is simply no calculating the extent of the grace we are to show.

In our world of private lives, we are prone to think that we may simply ignore offenses, or act outwardly friendly, without forgiving from the heart. But Jesus challenges us with his parable. The first servant has a debt that is astronomical and simply impossible to repay. However, the king forgives the whole thing. The second debtor owes just a little by comparison, but the first servant will not forgive. This provokes the king to reclaim the first servant and put him in prison. "Should not you have had mercy on your fellow servant, as I had mercy on you?" (v. 33). Jesus warns the disciples not to ignore this: "So also my heavenly Father will do to every one of you, if you do not forgive your brother from your heart" (v. 35).

Clearly God forgives every Christian beyond measure. We are destitute; we cannot possibly repay the debt we owe to God. He simply forgives generously and freely. That obliges us to offer the same kind of forgiveness to those who have injured us. If we remain unforgiving, God will not forgive our sins.

In a similar context, Jesus teaches that we are to go to reclaim our brother: "If your brother sins, rebuke him, and if he repents, forgive him, and if he sins against you seven times in the day, and turns to you seven times, saying, 'I repent,' you must forgive him" (Luke 17:3–4). Jesus requires reconciliation between servants in the kingdom. There is real sin in our relationships. We may not simply ignore it, but must realize that it is real. It does not please God to act as though "she did not mean it" or "it was nothing." Nor may we allow ourselves to become embittered toward each other. Paul writes, "If one has a complaint against another, forgiving each other; as the Lord has forgiven you, so you also must forgive" (Col. 3:13). It is simply not an option.

We can see how important this is in the church from the discipline that the Lord exercised on the church in Corinth. They came to the Lord's Supper without discerning the meaning of the body and blood of Christ. We know that the actions of some were demeaning to the poor in the church. The apostle warns us not to eat and drink judgment to ourselves as some of the Corinthian believers did.

What then should we do today? We should ask ourselves honestly, before God, whether there is someone toward whom we harbor resentment and bitterness. Is there a person who has offended you, or somehow hurt you, whom you have not forgiven? You can tell pretty well about this by asking whether you are able to forget what they did. If there is someone who has sinned against you, as you come to the Lord's Table today, resolve in your heart before God to do whatever is required to be reconciled to your brother or sister. This may be very difficult to face, but God will help you. If you must go to the person and bring it up, then you must, in all humility. You may need to ask for the help of a mature believer (one who will not "take sides") to encourage you and give perspective to the discussion (see Matt. 18:15–20).

On the other hand, there may be someone whom *you* have offended. It is your responsibility, in Christ, to go to him and ask his forgiveness. Most of all, ask yourself, "How much has God forgiven me? Does he withhold forgiveness from me?" and allow the answer to lead you to your brother.

Today, God will seal to your heart your union with Jesus Christ. He died for the forgiveness of your sins. Know that God in his lavish love has forgiven you. And receive strength from Christ to bring about and maintain reconciliation with your brothers and sisters in the kingdom. All this is the new covenant in his blood.

CHRIST'S POSSESSION IN BODY AND SOUL
— *1 Corinthians 6:20* —

There are sins that knock us down. Sexual sins are uniquely like that (see 1 Cor. 6:18). In Corinth the believers needed to be warned against prostitution, very much part of that city's culture. The apostle persuades in an amazing way. He says that the believers' bodies are members of Christ. Therefore their bodies may not be joined to a prostitute, because that would "involve" Christ. "Shall I then take the members of Christ and make them members of a prostitute? Never!" (v. 15). Not just our souls, but also our bodies are essential to our service of Christ. The coming bodily resurrection speaks of the importance of bodily behavior to God. "God raised the Lord and will also raise us up by his power" (v. 14; cf. 2 Cor. 5:10). Paul concludes chapter 6 by writing, "Do you not know that your body is a temple of the Holy Spirit within you, whom you have from God? You are not your own, for you were bought with a price. So glorify God in your body" (vv. 19–20). We do not have authority, ultimately, over our bodies. Christ does, because he purchased us.

How is it that we are one with Christ bodily? It is not a physical union as such. In his true humanity, Christ is in heaven and will remain there until his return. Christ's glorified human nature does not dwell in our bodies. So our union with Christ is not a bodily union like that of husband and wife. How then can Paul say that our bodies are "members" of Christ? He can say this because the Holy Spirit dwells in each believer as in a temple. We are "one spirit with him" (v. 17, see also v. 19). But there is another step in Paul's thinking. That is, the Holy Spirit is the Spirit of the glorious Lord Jesus Christ. Following his death, at his resurrection and glorification in heaven, Christ received a new relationship with the Holy Spirit. Later in the letter, Paul writes, "The last Adam became a life-giving Spirit" (1 Cor. 15:45).[16] This is a complex idea, but the gist of it is that the

---

16 Paul does not blur the distinction between the second and third persons of the Trinity. Instead he refers to the life-giving work of the Spirit as Christ's work. For more on this passage, see Richard B. Gaffin Jr., "Life-Giving Spirit: Probing the Center of Paul's Pneumatology," *Journal of the Evangelical Theological Society* 41, no. 4 (December 1998): 573–98, and his "The Last Adam, the Life-Giving Spirit," in *The Forgotten Christ: Exploring the Majesty and Mystery of God Incarnate*, ed. Stephen Clark (Nottingham, UK: Inter-Varsity Press, 2007), 191–231.

Spirit now, on earth, is the one who carries out Christ's ministry in the church and in each Christian. The Spirit's ministry is inseparable from Christ's. That is why Paul can move so easily in this passage from the idea of our bodies being members of Christ to our bodies as temples of the Holy Spirit.[17]

This is something like the relationship between the bread and wine of the Lord's Supper and Jesus' glorified human nature. His body and blood remain in heaven. But, as the glorified Christ, the Spirit is not separate from him. Christ's ministry is his ministry.

The Spirit graciously uses bread and wine as sign and seal to communicate to us our union with Christ. Therefore we should say that Christ communicates his union with us by the bread and wine. Christ's flesh is not in the bread, because he has ascended to heaven. But his Spirit is in you, and thus Christ is in you, and you have true fellowship with him in his whole person as you eat and drink.

Christ is not separated from the Spirit. They are one God. The Spirit dwells in you. Therefore, when you act immorally, you "take Christ along" with you. This must never be! Now, Paul does not condemn the Corinthian believers for their sexual sins. It may be difficult for us to grasp, but the blood of Christ cleanses from all sins, even these sins. We are to believe God about this. There are no outstanding, unforgiven sins of believers.

Paul does not condemn, but he does emphatically warn.

Flee from sexual immorality. (v. 18)

Do you not know that the unrighteous will not inherit the kingdom of God? Do not be deceived: neither the sexually

---

17 Paul writes something very similar in Romans 8:9–10: "Anyone who does not have the Spirit of Christ does not belong to him. But if Christ is in you, although the body is dead because of sin, the Spirit is life because of righteousness." Notice the way in which Paul refers interchangeably to "the Spirit of Christ," "Christ," and "the Spirit," each indwelling the mortal body of the believer.

immoral, nor idolaters, nor adulterers, nor men who practice homosexuality, nor thieves, nor the greedy, nor drunkards, nor revilers, nor swindlers will inherit the kingdom of God. And such were some of you. But you were washed, you were sanctified, you were justified in the name of the Lord Jesus Christ and by the Spirit of our God. (vv. 9–11)

The beautiful conclusion is that Christ gave his life as the ransom price for us: "You are not your own, for you were bought with a price. So glorify God in your body" (vv. 19–20).

Your body belongs to Jesus Christ, who purchased it. Jesus Christ lives in you. Today, eat this bread, Christ's body, and drink this cup, the new covenant in his blood, as the renewal of God's promise that Christ dwells in you. Call on the Lord for cleansing, and trust the God of all grace to cleanse and to strengthen you by the power of the Spirit, that you too may glorify God in your body.

God Is Faithful
— *1 Corinthians 10:13* —

As he did Israel in the wilderness, God feeds and protects us. We too are "a pilgrim people." As new-covenant believers, those "on whom the end of the ages has come" (1 Cor. 10:11), we eat and drink at the Table as our Lord provides food for us. Israel had manna and water from the rock to teach them to depend on him. They were completely dependent on this food and water for everyday life. We have the true bread of heaven, Jesus Christ. Here he feeds us.

We live under conditions like the wilderness generation did: the desert is a place of testing; it was hard going. We can say that the church lives in the wilderness. The church in Corinth was tested because allegiance to Christ challenged some dearly held practices in their world. Roman culture was very tolerant of religions. But here was Christ, wrote Paul, calling for allegiance to him alone. Christians could no longer eat meat offered in idol temples, because that would be to participate in idolatry. This posed a great challenge. If you were a servant or were dependent in some other way, but now refused hospitality by refusing to eat meat offered to idols, all sorts of hardship could come your way. If you would not participate in "partying" as you used to, you would become an outsider in the view of a very immoral, sexual culture. No doubt there was all manner of trouble that followed believers when they refused these occasions. Such tests pose temptations to us as well.

But Paul's assurance was there for them: the God who called them into fellowship with Christ (1 Cor. 1:9) is still "faithful, and he will not let you be tempted beyond your ability, but with the temptation he will also provide the way of escape, that you may be able to endure it" (v. 13). Your temptations are not new, and they are not irresistible. God has absolute control over the circumstances of your life. He promises that no temptation can come to you that is impossible to face. Call out to God for help—keep calling out to him. He is able and willing to rescue you, either by giving you endurance or by removing you from the situation. You may have to flee (v. 14).

We are in the position of weakness and need, which is always the true place of God's people in the world. What does he want us to do? He wants us to give thanks, to trust, to pray, and to obey the Word. The writer to the Hebrews says, "Let us then with confidence draw near to the throne of grace, that we may receive mercy and find grace to help in time of need" (Heb. 4:16). We need strength and forgiveness. Those are exactly the things that God provides in Christ. All who come to God through this High Priest find grace in time of need. This Table speaks of the same Christ: "This cup is the new covenant in my blood" (1 Cor. 11:25), "shed for many for the remission of sins" (Matt. 26:28 kjv). He is present with us in mighty power. The Spirit grants us fellowship with the ascended Christ here.

Christ strengthens us to bear up under temptation. But he does not give a "pass" to the willfully rebellious. That was Paul's warning to the Corinthians (vv. 6, 11).

What can provoke the Lord's jealousy? That may seem like a foolish question to us as people under grace. But Paul actually asked the Corinthians whether they were willing to try it (v. 22)! They were God's new-covenant people and, like Israel in the wilderness, they received baptism and the nourishment of Spiritual food. Paul described Israel's privileges in terms of the Christian sacraments: "Our fathers," he writes, "all were baptized into Moses" (vv. 1–2)—they were delivered through the Red Sea by the glory of God. All of them "drank the same [S]piritual[18] drink. For they drank from the [S]piritual Rock that followed them, and the Rock was Christ" (v. 4). Even before his incarnation in the fullness of time, Christ and the Spirit were present with his covenant people. Christ has always been the Savior of his people, in the Old Testament as well as in the New. What is "new" is that, for the Corinthians and for us, "the end of the ages has come" (v. 11). The great fulfillment of all the promises of God has come about in Christ's coming.

Like us, our fathers had privileges: baptism, the Word, the presence of Christ—in other words, the Spiritual nourishment of the means of grace. Like us, they had not yet arrived in the sworn land. They were subject to temptation and testing. God tested them for their good, as Satan tempted them to sin. Sadly, "most of them" (v. 5) failed to please God, and they came under judgment. Paul lists a number of judgments that were brought on members of the covenant community (vv. 7–10). Presumptuous idolatry, fornication, grumbling—these,

---

18 I have capitalized the adjective "Spiritual" to remind us that Paul is referring to the Holy Spirit.

without repentance, brought judgment. These things were written for our benefit.[19]

It was not sin, as such, that led to so many "falling" in the desert. Everyone commits sin. It was something more: verse 6 says that they "craved evil things."[20] That plural noun, "evil things," indicates that they were sinning presumptuously, persistently, and willfully.[21] This is confirmed by verse 9: "We must not put Christ to the test, as some of them did." To test God is to sin intentionally to see what God will do. The gospel promise of grace is made to a humble people, not to the presumptuous. So Paul writes, "Let anyone who thinks that he stands take heed lest he fall" (v. 12). It is good to be confident in the Lord, but not good to be confident in ourselves! When we sin, the Spirit convicts our hearts and leads us to repentance, faith, and forgiveness. But when we sin persistently and presumptuously, there is the terrible danger of God's judgment. That is true for us as it was true for Israel in the wilderness. No believer can be lost. But, by the Spirit's work in grace, no believer will continue to test the Lord.

Christ the Lord is completely sufficient for all our need, both for forgiveness and for strength. Receive the bread of heaven from the Lord of heaven today. Eat his body by faith. Drink the cup of the new covenant in Christ's blood, shed for you. Receive the assurance that God is faithful. He "will not let you be tempted beyond your ability, but with the temptation he will also provide the way of escape, that you may be able to endure it."

---

19 This instruction, and indeed warning, are fully compatible with God's unchangeable purpose to save his elect. In fact, warning is one of the *means* God uses to preserve our faith. See the Canons of Dort, Fifth Head of Doctrine, article 14: "And, just as it has pleased God to begin this work of grace in us, so he preserves, continues, and completes his work by the hearing and reading of the gospel, by meditation on it, by its exhortations, threats, and promises, and also by the use of the sacraments."

20 My translation. The ESV has "desire," but the verb ἐπεθύμησαν (*epethumēsan*) is much stronger.

21 A point made by Dr. Richard Gaffin in his class at Westminster Theological Seminary, "The Theology of Hebrews."

ONE BREAD, ONE BODY
— *1 Corinthians 10:16–17* —

When we eat the bread, we partake of Christ's body. When we drink the cup, we partake of Christ's blood. The New Testament presents the Lord's Table as a church meal. The whole church participates together. Paul stresses this: "Because there is one bread, we who are many are one body, for we all partake of the one bread" (1 Cor. 10:17).[22] The single loaf of bread is a sign that we are united to Christ. In other words, together we are one, because each of us is in him. We are nourished together. We grow together.

Being one body means that we are bound to each other. The church is a family (though we still live in our own families). We are a family of families (even though our possessions and family structures are not merged into one[23]). We must recognize that we are connected to each other because we are one with the Lord. This is a profound union.

In Corinth some of the wealthier members humiliated the poor by eating the Lord's Supper alone, excluding from their table those who had nothing. That was rude and scandalous. Paul corrected it. Apparently others were participating somehow in non-Christian religious activities. Probably they were eating meat that had been sacrificed to a pagan idol. Paul reminds them that they joined in with demons as well as with unbelievers (v. 20)! Some of the Corinthian believers, rightly understanding that there is only one true God, and that no idol "is anything" (v. 19), were eating without thinking about the consciences of others. There was nothing tainted about the food, because all the fullness of the earth belongs to Christ (v. 26). But

---

22 Jesus' identification of the cup as "the new covenant in my blood" (1 Cor. 11:25) has an identical corporate meaning, because a covenant is made with a whole covenant *people*.

23 When believers gave their possessions generously to relieve the poor in the book of Acts, they did so freely. See Acts 5:3–5.

eating was a corporate event, and Paul made certain that, if the meat was identified as having been sacrificed, believers abstain from eating. This prohibition was not for their consciences' sake, but for the sake of the person who so identified it (vv. 28–29). In other words, your freedom to eat is limited by danger to the other person's conscience. If he believes it is sinful, skip it, so he is not tempted to sin. Eating, drinking (and everything else in life!), is not just for me, but for God's glory and for the good of the church and the neighbor (v. 31).

What do we receive in the fellowship of the body of Christ? We receive Christ's gifts, the gifts of the Spirit. These gifts are given by the various members of the body for our good. Our pastors teach us the Word of God and live it out, as examples to the flock. We teach it to each other. One friend is strong and wise, offering insight to help sort out the path God would have us take. Another is kind and knows how to accept us through the highs and lows of our walk. Yet another is down-to-earth and shows the wisdom of everyday prayer and obedience. Another is humble and does not see his many accomplishments as reasons for pride. Still another has the ability and kindness to connect with unbelievers to show them the love of Christ. There are those with vision for the growth of the ministry. Another shows great patience. All of us have been forgiven much by the Lord and by the brothers and sisters. A young person has great joy in Christ. Another, who could never speak in public, is so solid that she could not possibly be moved away from her example of godliness. Some help us to sing. Some show what it means to give liberally. Still others show us faithfulness by serving in the midst of their own sufferings. Others are weaker and need encouragement. When we receive, we grow; when we give, we grow. We learn Christ together. We suffer together. We rejoice together. We live and we die together. The apostles are our teachers. Christ is our Lord, and God is our Father. Our eating at this Table is a meal *together*. If our behavior has created a stumbling block for someone's faith, we must remove it. If we have received offense, we may not allow bitterness to grow, but again must take measures to restore the peace.[24] If a member of the body needs help, love may not ignore that need. Paul writes, "Let no one seek his own good, but the good of his neighbor" (v. 24). If there is praise to be given, we must give it—likewise a necessary rebuke. How deeply God loves his church!

Beloved, let us give profound thanks for the body of Christ. As we eat this bread and drink the cup of thanksgiving, let us rejoice in each other. For Christ's body, given for us, and his blood shed for us, have made us one in him.

He Bore Our Sins
— *1 Peter 2:24* —

Peter writes to believers who are suffering unjustly. He wants them to follow Jesus' example. Jesus did not retaliate or revile. Do not fight back when you are treated unjustly—this is a "gracious thing" (1 Peter 2:20).

This is the path of discipleship. Because of the immense grace of God to you in Christ, do not fight back. Endure unjust suffering, as Christ did. Bear witness to the grace of God. To this you have been called (v. 21). We are to do this on account of Christ's saving example. Peter takes the words of Isaiah 53 (vv. 4–6, 9, 11–12) and shows how Jesus Christ fulfilled them. These are Old Testament words, inspired in the prophets by "the Spirit of Christ" (1 Peter 1:11–12).

---

24 Hear Calvin's eloquence: "We will have benefited much from the sacrament if this knowledge is engraved and imprinted within our hearts: that we cannot wound, slander, mock, despise, or in any way offend any of the brethren without at the same time wounding, slandering, mocking, despising or offending Jesus Christ in them; we cannot have quarrels or divisions with our brothers without quarreling with and being divided from Jesus Christ; we cannot love Jesus Christ without loving him in our brothers" (*Institutes of the Christian Religion: 1541 French Edition*, trans. Elsie Anne McKie [Grand Rapids: Eerdmans, 2009], 563–64). Cf. his statement in 1559; *Inst.*, 2:1415–16 (4/17.38).

Christ was meek before Herod and Pilate; he did not threaten or retaliate. You and I are to accept opposition without cursing our enemies. We do it because God shows grace to us, and we return that grace to others.

Christ is the pattern. But is Christ just an example of courage, like many others we might think of? It is not as if anyone who does not retaliate against unjust treatment can be just as much an example. Christ is much more than an inspiring figure like Gandhi. Christ's suffering is our model because we are one with him and because he atoned for our sins. Because he died for our sins, we live a new life; we "live to righteousness." Peter writes this in verse 24: "He himself bore our sins in his body on the tree, that we might die to sin and live to righteousness. By his wounds you have been healed." His sacrifice transforms our lives.

Christ suffered the punishment of God as a substitute in our place. "He himself bore our sins in his body on the tree." (Peter refers to the cross of Christ as "the tree," thinking of Deuteronomy 21:23, where God's curse is called down on one who is hung on a tree.)

How was this "bearing" of our sins accomplished? The only way that Christ could have borne our sins was by accepting the judgment against sin and by assuming the consequence: death. The apostle is expounding here the suffering Servant of Isaiah 53:4–6.

Surely he has borne our griefs
    and carried our sorrows;
yet we esteemed him stricken,
    smitten by God, and afflicted.
But he was wounded for our transgressions;
    he was crushed for our iniquities;
upon him was the chastisement that brought us peace,
    and with his wounds we are healed.
All we like sheep have gone astray;

we have turned—every one—to his own way;
and the Lord has laid on him
the iniquity of us all.

Our liability was borne by Christ. The sins were borne by means of the Servant being bruised, struck, and afflicted. The nature of sin bearing was a matter of punishment. The punishment was of divine origin. It was accomplished for others. The suffering of the victim resulted in healing. His sufferings were a sacrifice that made full satisfaction for sin, according to the will of God.[25]

But notice too that Christ accepted suffering and death voluntarily. "He did not threaten, but continued entrusting himself to him who judges justly" (1 Peter 2:23).

The bread and wine of this sacrament seal on your hearts God's provision for you. We need grace, strength, and, often, to love very difficult people. Christ bore our sins so that our vengeance might die and we might live to righteousness. It is what God intended. Receive these gifts, eat and drink today, as they seal God's Christ to you. Feed on him in your heart by faith, with thanksgiving.

Until I Drink It New with You
— *Matthew 26:28–29* —

In these words, Jesus brings together two certainties: his sufferings and his future glory. In only a few hours the last sacrifice of covenant blood will be offered on the cross. The prophecy that "he poured out his soul to death" (Isa. 53:12) will be fulfilled. Jesus knew exactly the purpose of his death for our sins. His death would inaugurate the new covenant promised by Jeremiah, in which God's people would now know him and he would forgive their sins completely (Jer. 31:31–34).

---

25 Paul Wells explains the logic of the passage in *Cross Words: The Biblical Doctrine of the Atonement* (Ross-Shire, UK: Christian Focus, 2006), 144–45.

His sufferings were real and were much too great for us fully to grasp. But Jesus faced his death with absolute *certainty* of his resurrection and exaltation. His death would bring about the final coming of God's kingdom. God's final order for the creation, predicted by the prophets (and already begun in his ministry), would then be secured. Jesus referred to the meal this way: "until it is fulfilled in the kingdom of God" (Luke 22:16).[26] Jesus was quite certain that this would come. It must come, because, through his sacrifice, God would not fail to bring about all the promises of the new covenant. That final kingdom will include nothing less than the salvation of sinners and the renewal of the entire cosmos.

Jesus' words about the wine, "until . . . I drink it *new* with you" (Matt. 26:29), speak of the renewal of the cosmos at his return. What will it be? Not drunkenness but rejoicing in a new heavens and earth, at the feast, with the finest wine (Isa. 25:6–8). In Genesis, Jacob prophesied to Judah that when Shiloh came, the King from his line, he would sit on his throne; because there would be such abundance, he would be able to wash his garments with wine (Gen. 49:10–11).

Jesus changed water into wine at the wedding in Cana (John 2:1–11). The hour of his death and resurrection had not yet come, but he gave a sign of the abundance of the Messiah's wedding feast. There were six stone jars there, each holding twenty or thirty gallons. (Think of the size of your gas tank.) He created the very best wine, saved for last, in vast amounts—between 120 and 180 gallons! There will be no famine in the new heavens and new earth. Like Cana's sign, Jesus' miracles of feeding thousands were signs of the abundance that his kingdom will bring, because the curse will finally be removed from the creation. Paul tells us,

---

26 Jesus referred to the Passover meal as it would be fulfilled in the messianic banquet. He then institutes the Supper, which also anticipates the banquet.

Christ redeemed us from the curse of the law by becoming a curse for us—for it is written, "Cursed is everyone who is hanged on a tree"—so that in Christ Jesus the blessing of Abraham might come to the Gentiles, so that we might receive the promised Spirit through faith. (Gal. 3:13–14)

Jesus' death brought about the outpouring of the Spirit. The Spirit has brought salvation to Jew and Gentile alike. Therefore the banquet on that day will include believers gathered from all the earth. Jew and Gentile will eat together with Abraham, Isaac, and Jacob (Matt. 8:11). All the saints together, in resurrected glory, will eat and drink with Jesus at his table in his kingdom.

Perhaps most wondrous of all is Jesus' promise to those who await his return and serve him faithfully. They lived for him and trusted their heavenly Father to provide for them. Their Lord went away to "the wedding feast," Jesus says (Luke 12:36–37), referring to his own ascension and the joyous reception of heaven. But when he returns and knocks on the door, "Blessed are those servants whom the master finds awake when he comes. Truly, I say to you, he will dress himself for service and have them recline at table, *and he will come and serve them*" (v. 37). It is just fine to be a doorkeeper in the house of God! Shouldn't we serve *him* on that day? Of course we will. It is truly beyond our ability to grasp that, then, the Lord who died for us will serve us. What wonder! The second person of the Holy Trinity—eternal, glorious Son, now exalted to God's right hand—will serve us. Oh, the joy of that day! It seems too good to be true! We love him and long to see him. This is the greatness of his love. Truly, "No eye has seen, nor ear heard, nor the heart of man imagined, what God has prepared for those who love him" (1 Cor. 2:9). Only the total transformation of resurrection glory, greater than anything we now imagine, will make us able to receive such joy! Glory!

"Until . . . I drink it new with you." Jesus awaits that day! Why? Not on account of some lack—but he waits for the feast because he has planned to have that joy only together with his church. The Bridegroom can truly rejoice only with his bride.

The greatest joy on that great day will be his presence. When the disciples saw the resurrected Christ, they "took hold of his feet and worshiped him" (Matt. 28:9). We will see him, our Savior and Lord, face to face. Then we will be like him (1 John 3:1–2). For now, we have a kind of seeing that is called "believing." We love him, and we rejoice with joy inexpressible and filled with glory (1 Peter 1:8). We believe his promises. We are forgiven. We know his love for us. It is just a small beginning, but what an ending there will be! Eat and drink the bread and wine of the kingdom feast to come. "Drink of it, all of you, for this is my blood of the covenant, which is poured out for many for the forgiveness of sins" (Matt. 26:27–28). Soon the day will come when he will drink with you, *anew*, in his Father's kingdom.

THE MARRIAGE SUPPER OF THE LAMB
— *Revelation 19:6–10* —

On the last day, when God's judgment is complete, the great throng of the saints will raise their voices in glorious praise. John heard the sound, "like the roar of many waters and like the sound of mighty peals of thunder" (Rev. 19:6). Their combined voices make such a great sound, probably because they are echoing the mighty voice of God himself. They press each other to be exceedingly glad because God has finished his work of judgment. Now the full realization of his covenant has come. "The marriage of the Lamb has come" (v. 7).

God has removed "Babylon" from the earth. Since the days of Israel, Babylon, the world system that put itself in God's place, has made life difficult for God's people. "Hallelujah! For the Lord our

God the Almighty reigns [or *has begun to reign*[27]]" (v. 6). But if God has always been sovereign in his world, what can this "beginning" be? It is the beginning of God's eternal reign in the new heavens and earth, the creation now cleansed from all evil. This omega point of God's decree has been in his view since before the creation of the universe—God's full glory, given to his Son and expressed in his world, in the midst of his glorified congregation.

In the West, believers do not feel the heat of oppressive governments like Christians in other places do. But we all labor under constant temptation from the world. Indeed every struggle has a purpose in God's wisdom. "Babylon" is exactly the fire that God uses to refine his saints.

The bride has made herself ready. God granted that she should be clothed with fine linen. God will reward the perseverance of his people with "fine linen, bright and pure" (vv. 7–8). These are the saints' "righteous deeds." Of course, from the beginning to the end of God's plan, all these are his gracious gifts. They are the good works for which he has created them (Eph. 2:8–10).

This wonderful clothing shows the beauty of Christ, our Savior. Those who receive the white robes are the same ones who, earlier in Revelation, have "washed . . . in the blood of the Lamb" (7:14; see also 1:5). Christ's blood brought forgiveness and the power of the Spirit to overcome temptation at last (12:11; 19:13).

On the last day we will have the joy of the bride. God will reward us, and we will rejoice in that reward without boasting or self-assertion (something we struggle with today). God delights in our obedience to him. We will delight along with him in his reward. At the center of all will be Christ, "the Lamb," who purchased us with his blood. Every bit of it is the fruit of his free grace. We will all rejoice together. But

---

27 Gregory K. Beale argues that the verb is an "ingressive aorist" (*The Book of Revelation: A Commentary on the Greek Text*, The New International Greek Testament Commentary, ed. I. Howard Marshall and Donald A. Hagner [Grand Rapids: Eerdmans, 1999], 931).

their clothes cannot be considered white until each member has completed the process of perseverance.[28] For now, we must strive against the world, the flesh, and the Devil.

But there is more. We are called "the bride of the Lamb." The personal, tender picture is that of the happiness of bride and bridegroom. God's promise to Hosea will finally be fulfilled: "I will betroth you to me forever. I will betroth you to me in righteousness and in justice, in steadfast love and in mercy. I will betroth you to me in faithfulness. And you shall know the LORD" (Hos. 2:19–20). All our waiting will be over. The delight of our hearts, now separated from us because he is in heavenly glory, will have come to receive us to himself. You have yearned for that moment. It will come soon. And from that moment on, you will know only more and more of the love of Father, Son, and Holy Spirit. This is the blessing that God has in store for the whole church. Our great prize will be that we reflect the very glory of Christ. We will be the "bride adorned for her husband" (21:2), "having the glory of God" (21:11). Beloved, you will soon gather at that feast. Today, eat this bread and drink this cup as the foretaste of that joyful, blessed meal. Receive Christ again, who is your strength to continue the battle. Jesus Christ overcame. He will fight for you and enable you to overcome. Soon you will sing with a voice like mighty peals of thunder, "Hallelujah! For the Lord our God the Almighty reigns." "Blessed are those who are invited to the marriage supper of the Lamb. . . . These are the true words of God" (19:9).

---

28 Ibid., 944.

Bibliography

Augustine, Saint. *Confessions: A New Translation by Henry Chadwick.* Oxford World's Classics. New York: Oxford University Press, 1992.

———. "Tractate 80 on John 15:1–3." In *Nicene and Post-Nicene Fathers.* 1st series, vol. 7, edited by Philip Schaff, 343–45. Grand Rapids: Eerdmans, 1956.

Bavinck, Herman. *Our Reasonable Faith.* Translated by Henry Zylstra. Grand Rapids: Eerdmans, 1956.

———. *Reformed Dogmatics.* Vol. 2, *God and Creation.* Edited by John Bolt. Translated by John Vriend. Grand Rapids: Baker Academic, 2004.

———. *Reformed Dogmatics.* Vol. 3, *Sin and Salvation in Christ.* Edited by John Bolt. Translated by John Vriend. Grand Rapids: Baker Academic, 2006.

———. *Reformed Dogmatics.* Vol. 4, *Holy Spirit, Church, and New Creation.* Edited by John Bolt. Translated by John Vriend. Grand Rapids: Baker Academic, 2008.

Beale, Gregory K. *The Book of Revelation: A Commentary on the Greek Text.* The New International Greek Testament Commentary, edited by I. Howard Marshall and Donald A. Hagner. Grand Rapids: Eerdmans, 1999.

Berkouwer, G. C. *The Sacraments.* Translated by Hugo Bekker. Studies in Dogmatics. Grand Rapids: Eerdmans, 1969.

Blocher, Henri. *Songs of the Servant: Isaiah's Good News.* London: Inter-Varsity Press, 1975.

Blocher, Henri A.G. "Calvin on the Lord's Supper: Revisiting an Intriguing Diversity, Part 1." *Westminster Theological Journal* 76, no. 1 (2014): 55–93.

————. "Calvin on the Lord's Supper: Revisiting an Intriguing Diversity, Part 2." *Westminster Theological Journal* 76, no. 2 (2014): 411–29.

Blomberg, Craig. *Contagious Holiness: Jesus' Meals with Sinners*. New Studies in Biblical Theology 19, edited by D. A. Carson. Downers Grove, IL: InterVarsity Press, 2005.

Boston, Thomas. *Memoirs of Thomas Boston*. 1899. Reprint, Edinburgh: Banner of Truth, 1988.

Calvin, John. *Institutes of the Christian Religion*. Edited by John T. McNeill. Translated by Ford Lewis Battles. 2 vols. Library of Christian Classics 20–21. Philadelphia: Westminster, 1960.

————. *Institutes of the Christian Religion: 1541 French Edition*. Translated by Elsie A. McKee. Grand Rapids: Eerdmans, 2009.

————. *Short Treatise on the Lord's Supper*. Translated by J. K. S. Reid. Library of Christian Classics 22. Philadelphia: Westminster, 1954.

Carson, D. A. "Adumbrations of Atonement Theology in the Fourth Gospel." *Journal of the Evangelical Theological Society* 57, no. 3 (September 2014): 513–22.

————. "Atonement in Romans 3:21–26." In *The Glory of the Atonement: Biblical, Historical and Practical Perspectives; Essays in Honor of Roger Nicole*, edited by Charles E. Hill and Frank A. James III, 119–39. Downers Grove, IL: InterVarsity Press, 2004.

Catechism of the Catholic Church with Modifications from the Editio Typica. 2nd ed. New York: Doubleday, 1997.

Ciampa, Roy E., and Brian S. Rosner. *The First Letter to the Corinthians*. Edited by D. A. Carson. Grand Rapids: Eerdmans, 2010.

Clowney, Edmund P. *The Church*. Contours of Biblical Theology, edited by Gerald Bray. Downers Grove, IL: InterVarsity Press, 1994.

DeYoung, Kevin. *The Hole in Our Holiness: Filling the Gap between Gospel Passion and the Pursuit of Godliness.* Wheaton, IL: Crossway, 2012.

Fee, Gordon D. *The First Epistle to the Corinthians.* Grand Rapids: Eerdmans, 1987.

———. *Pauline Christology: An Exegetical-Theological Study.* Peabody, MA: Hendrickson, 2007.

Ferguson, Sinclair B. *The Holy Spirit.* Contours of Christian Theology, edited by Gerald S. Bray. Downers Grove, IL: InterVarsity Press, 1996.

———. "Preaching the Atonement." In *The Glory of the Atonement: Biblical, Historical and Practical Perspectives; Essays in Honor of Roger Nicole*, edited by Charles E. Hill and Frank A. James III, 426–43. Downers Grove, IL: InterVarsity Press, 2004.

———. "The Reformed View." In *Christian Spirituality: Five Views of Sanctification*, edited by Donald L. Alexander, 47–76. Downers Grove, IL: InterVarsity Press, 1988.

Frame, John M. *The Doctrine of the Word of God.* A Theology of Lordship. Phillipsburg, NJ: P&R Publishing, 2010.

Gaffin, Richard B., Jr. "Biblical Theology and the Westminster Standards." *Westminster Theological Journal* 65, no. 2 (2003): 165–79.

———. *By Faith, Not By Sight: Paul and the Order of Salvation.* 2nd ed. Phillipsburg, NJ: P&R Publishing, 2013.

———. "The Last Adam, the Life-Giving Spirit." In *The Forgotten Christ: Exploring the Majesty and Mystery of God Incarnate*, edited by Stephen Clark, 191–231. Nottingham, UK: Inter-Varsity Press, 2007.

———. "Life-Giving Spirit: Probing the Center of Paul's Pneumatology." *Journal of the Evangelical Theological Society* 41, no. 4 (December 1998): 573–98.

————. *Perspectives on Pentecost: New Testament Teaching on the Gifts of the Holy Spirit.* Phillipsburg, NJ: Presbyterian and Reformed, 1979.

————. *Resurrection and Redemption: A Study in Paul's Soteriology.* 1978. Reprint, Phillipsburg, NJ: Presbyterian and Reformed, 1987.

Garland, David E. *1 Corinthians.* Baker Exegetical Commentary on the New Testament, edited by Robert W. Yarbrough and Robert H. Stein. Grand Rapids: Baker Book House, 2003.

Goppelt, Leonhard. *Theology of the New Testament.* Vol. 2, *The Variety and Unity of the Apostolic Witness to Christ,* translated by John Alsup, edited by Jurgen Roloff. Grand Rapids: Eerdmans, 1982.

Grudem, Wayne. *Systematic Theology: An Introduction to Biblical Doctrine.* Grand Rapids: Zondervan, 1994.

Haight, Roger. "Sin and Grace." In *Systematic Theology: Roman Catholic Perspectives.* 2nd ed., edited by Francis S. Fiorenza and John P. Galvin, 375–430. Minneapolis: Fortress, 2011.

Hofius, Otfried. "The Lord's Supper and the Lord's Supper Tradition: Reflections on 1 Cor 11:23b–25." In *One Loaf, One Cup: Ecumenical Studies of 1 Cor 11 and Other Eucharistic Texts,* edited by Ben F. Meyer, 75–115. Macon, GA: Mercer University Press, 1993.

Hunsinger, George. *The Eucharist and Ecumenism: Let Us Keep the Feast.* Cambridge: Cambridge University Press, 2008.

Jeffery, Steve, Michael Ovey, and Andrew Sach. *Pierced for Our Transgressions: Rediscovering the Glory of Penal Substitution.* Wheaton, IL: Crossway, 2007.

Jeremias, Joachim. *The Eucharistic Words of Jesus.* Translated by Norman Perrin. 1977. Reprint, Philadelphia: Fortress, 1981. Page references are to the 1977 edition.

Kline, Meredith G. *Kingdom Prologue: Genesis Foundations for a Covenantal Worldview.* Overland Park, KS: Two Age Press, 2000.

Kloosterman, Nelson D. "Proverbs 22:6 and Covenant Succession." In *To You and Your Children: Examining the Biblical Doctrine of Covenant Succession,* edited by Benjamin K. Wikner, 29–58. Moscow, ID: Canon Press, 2005.

Letham, Robert. *The Lord's Supper: Eternal Word in Broken Bread.* Phillipsburg, NJ: P&R Publishing, 2001.

Macleod, Donald. *Christ Crucified: Understanding the Atonement.* Downers Grove, IL: InterVarsity Press, 2014.

Marcel, Pierre Charles. *In God's School: Foundations for a Christian Life.* Translated by Howard Griffith. Eugene, OR: Wipf & Stock, 2009.

Marshall, I. Howard. *Last Supper and Lord's Supper.* London: Paternoster, 1980. Reprint, Vancouver: Regent College, 2006. Page references are to the 2006 edition.

Metzger, Bruce M. *A Textual Commentary on the Greek New Testament.* New York: United Bible Societies, 1975.

Mid-America Reformed Seminary. *Ecumenical and Reformed Creeds and Confessions.* Orange City, IA: Mid-America Reformed Seminary, 1991.

Moo, Douglas J. *The Epistle to the Romans.* The New International Commentary on the New Testament, edited by Gordon D. Fee. Grand Rapids: Eerdmans, 1996.

Morris, Leon M. *The Apostolic Preaching of the Cross.* 1965. 3rd rev. ed, Grand Rapids: Eerdmans, 2000. Page references are to the 2000 edition.

Motyer, J. Alec. *The Prophecy of Isaiah: An Introduction and Commentary.* Downers Grove, IL: InterVarsity Press, 1993.

Murray, John. *Collected Writings of John Murray.* Vol. 2, *Systematic Theology,* edited by Iain H. Murray. Edinburgh: Bannner of Truth, 1977.

———. *Collected Writings of John Murray.* Vol. 3, *The Life of John Murray: Sermons and Reviews,* edited by Iain H. Murray. Edinburgh: Banner of Truth, 1982.

Old, Hughes Oliphant. *Holy Communion in the Piety of the Reformed Church.* Edited by Jon D. Payne. Powder Springs, GA: Tolle Lege Press, 2013.

Pennington, Jonathan T. "The Lord's Supper in the Fourfold Witness of the Gospels." In *The Lord's Supper: Remembering and Proclaiming Christ until He Comes,* edited by Thomas R. Schreiner and Matthew R. Crawford, 31–67. Nashville: B&H Academic, 2010.

Peterson, David G. *Encountering God Together: Leading Worship Services That Honor God, Minister to His People, and Build His Church.* Phillipsburg, NJ: P&R Publishing, 2013.

Poythress, Vern S. "Indifferentism and Rigorism in the Church: With Implications for Baptizing Small Children." *Westminster Theological Journal* 59, no. 1 (1997): 13–29. Available online at http://www.frame-poythress.org/indifferentism-and-rigorism/.

———. *Inerrancy and the Gospels: A God-Centered Approach to the Challenges of Harmonization.* Wheaton, IL: Crossway, 2012.

Ridderbos, Herman. *The Coming of the Kingdom.* Translated by H. de Jongste. Philadelphia: Presbyterian and Reformed, 1962.

———. *The Gospel of John: A Theological Commentary.* Translated by John Vriend. Grand Rapids: Eerdmans, 1997.

———. *Paul: An Outline of His Theology.* Translated by John R. deWitt. Grand Rapids: Eerdmans, 1975.

Robertson, O. Palmer. *The Christ of the Covenants.* Phillipsburg, NJ: Presbyterian and Reformed, 1980.

Thiselton, Anthony C. *The First Epistle to the Corinthians: A Commentary on the Greek Text.* The New International Greek Testament Commentary, edited by I. Howard Marshall and Donald A. Hagner. Grand Rapids: Eerdmans, 2000.

Turretin, Francis. *Institutes of Elenctic Theology.* Vol. 1, *First through Tenth Topics*, translated by George Musgrave Giger, edited by James T. Dennison Jr. Phillipsburg, NJ: P&R Publishing, 1992.

Venema, Cornelis P. *Children at the Lord's Table? Assessing the Case for Paedocommunion.* Grand Rapids: Reformation Heritage, 2009.

————. "The Doctrine of the Lord's Supper in the Reformed Confessions." *Mid-America Journal of Theology* 12 (2001): 135–99.

————. "The Doctrine of the Sacraments and Baptism in the Reformed Confessions." *Mid-America Journal of Theology* 11 (2000): 21–86.

Vos, Geerhardus. *Biblical Theology: Old and New Testaments.* Grand Rapids: Eerdmans, 1948. Reprint, Edinburgh: Banner of Truth, 1975. Citations refer to the reprint edition.

————. *Grace and Glory: Sermons Preached in the Chapel of Princeton Theological Seminary.* Edinburgh: Banner of Truth, 1994.

————. *The Kingdom of God and the Church*, reprinted with additions and corrections. Nutley, NJ: Presbyterian and Reformed, 1972.

Waltke, Bruce K. *Genesis: A Commentary.* Grand Rapids: Zondervan, 2000.

Wells, Paul. *Cross Words: The Biblical Doctrine of the Atonement.* Ross-Shire, UK: Christian Focus, 2006.